Ichiro on Ichiro

ICHIRO
ON ICHIRO

CONVERSATIONS WITH NARUMI KOMATSU

Translated by Philip Gabriel

SASQUATCH BOOKS
SEATTLE

Printed in Canada
Published by Sasquatch Books
Distributed by Publishers Group West
12 11 10 09 08 07 06 05 04   6 5 4 3 2 1

Book design: Stewart A. Williams
Cover photograph: ©Duomo/Corbis
Interior photographs: frontispiece, x-1, 42, 58-59, 72, 84-85, 114-115, 144-145, 191, 200-201, and 231 by Ben VanHouten.

Library of Congress Cataloging-in-Publication Data

Suzuki, Ichiro, 1973-
     Ichiro on Ichiro : conversations with Narumi Komatsu / translated by Philip Gabriel.
     p.   cm.
     ISBN 1-57061-431-8
        1. Suzuki, Ichiro, 1973—Interviews. 2. Baseball players—United States—Interviews.   I. Komatsu, Narumi. II. Title.

GV865.S895A3 2004
796.357'092—dc22
[B]
                              2004045443

Sasquatch Books / 119 South Main Street, Suite 400 / Seattle, WA 98104
(206) 467-4300 / www.sasquatchbooks.com / custserv@sasquatchbooks.com

CONTENTS

PREFACE

This book contains interviews with Ichiro Suzuki made during a long period of time. I was fortunate to have the chance to talk with the Japanese major leaguer in Seattle just a few days after he was announced as the American League MVP (Most Valuable Player) award winner of the 2001 season. This interview is the basis for the first chapter of the book. During this interview he generously shared with me his memories of his first year in major-league baseball. His insight and analytical spirit haven't changed a bit since his days in Japan. Since I first met him in 1999 we have had more than 36 hours of discussions. Most of those talks form the basis of the rest of the book. There are many insights into his childhood, since the days his father gave him his first glove, up until he came to play for the Mariners.

If American readers find this book of interest, this is very much owed to Ichiro's eloquence and passion for the game. I also would like to thank Ichiro Suzuki's wife, Yumiko Suzuki, who was always at his side during these interviews and kindly answered those questions directed to her. I am much indebted to Mr. Philip Gabriel, who did such a wonderful job translating this book into English, and also to Mr. Brad Lefton, who supervised this book and the translation, sharing his knowledge of both Ichiro and major-league baseball.

Narumi Komatsu

CHAPTER ONE

LIFE IN THE MAJORS

Winning the MVP

In 2001 you finally became a major leaguer, and you must have had all kinds of experiences you never would have imagined when you were in Japan.

It's been such a dizzying experience ever since I joined the Mariners. Sometimes it feels like several years have gone by, and sometimes like it's just been a few months. It's the most dramatic change I've ever gone through.

Since you joined the Mariners, fans in Japan have been able to really experience how great major-league baseball is—through satellite broadcasts of games from the U.S. Watching you play has brought the major leagues much closer to home for the Japanese, though they continue to be amazed by major-league ballplayers' running, hitting, and defense—the high level of play in the majors. People in Japan have been so excited watching you, and the other Japanese players in the majors, that news about the major leagues is now more popular than news about Japanese professional baseball.

I think it's great they can enjoy the major leagues so much. The whole experience has been as surprising and exciting for me as for people in Japan who've been rooting for me. I've always dreamed of playing in the majors, and to be able to do so now is a real thrill.

In November of 2000 you left Japan and began your major-league career when you joined the Mariners in their training camp in Peoria, Arizona. Looking back on it, what particular scene stands out in your mind?

What I remember most wasn't the first time I stood in the ballpark for a game, but the time when the Orix Blue Wave, one of the twelve Japanese pro baseball teams, of which I was still a member, announced that I was being posted so I could officially enter the major leagues—when the bids were in and the Mariners were announced as the team winning the right to negotiate for me. Maybe I remember that time because it was the most stressful. All I could think about was major-league baseball. After a month of spring training we started the season, and I could finally start to feel—a little, at least—that I was playing again. It was fun waiting for the decision about the posting, but I was worried, too. I couldn't imagine all the things that have happened since then. It's definitely been dramatic—the changes in lifestyle, in my surroundings.

Before the 2001 season began, when you were in the spring training camp in Peoria, you said, "I don't have any friends here and the only way I can relax is to go for a drive." And your wife, Yumiko, said, "Even just going shopping for food, everything's different from in Japan. And it's not easy to get the kind of tasty meat and fresh fish we're used to enjoying back home."

I decided to go after my dream, and went for it. And Yumiko did everything she could to back me up. The only way to overcome my concerns was to forge ahead. Maybe that's why I remember that period so well, because that's the sort of time it was.

Making the move to Seattle and deciding to join the Mariners and live in a different culture maybe brought out a different kind of strength from when you lived in Japan?

I had to adapt, to learn to live in an environment completely different from what I was used to, which naturally wasn't easy. I had to learn to accept it all—the different rules, customs, food, language—you name it. But I didn't find it all that painful a transition. I knew I had to adapt to these differences and live in Seattle if I wanted to play ball in the U.S.

Along with these mental aspects, hasn't your baseball technique also progressed and been transformed since you came to the States? You were the top batter for seven years in Japan, but you've evolved over this year in the U.S. The records you set and the awards you've received are certainly proof of this.

Certainly I had to play a new role compared to when I was in Japan, and I had to perform if the team was going to win. In that sense, technique, and the records, too, were on an upward curve.

Did the high level of play here, which was much more than you imagined, spur you on to improve your own play?

It did. I gained the confidence that if I played up to my ability I'd be able to make out OK, but beyond that I experienced how really intense and amazing major-league baseball can be. Another thing I could feel up close was the unexpected unity Americans showed after the terrorist attacks of September 11. I never would have experienced that if I hadn't been part of the major leagues.

And all of these experiences you could take out into the field with you and put into "play."

Absolutely.

The culmination of all this was winning the American League MVP award. How did you feel when you heard you'd won it, back on November 20?

I heard about it in a phone call to my house. I'd just woken up and had switched on my computer to check my e-mails when the phone rang. It was from Hidenori Sueyoshi of the Mariners. "Congratulations," he told me. "You just won the MVP!" I was still half asleep and said something like "What?" I managed to thank him, but it still hadn't really hit me.

As you woke up more, then, the reality of the situation must have sunk in.

Once I was fully awake it hit me, and I thought, "Wow! This is something!" I was so excited I couldn't sit still. I really hadn't been thinking about the MVP at all. I was sure all the time that my teammate Bret Boone would win it. He'd set a record [for second basemen] that season of 141 RBIs. Plus he'd hit a lot of game-winning hits. I figured Boone was the best man for the MVP, so I was actually pretty surprised when my name came up as a candidate.

Boone's great season was reported pretty extensively in Japan, and people learned all about him—the fact, for instance, that he's a third-generation major leaguer. I wonder if having you on the team might have been the impetus to his great season.

He must have thought he didn't want to lose out to the new guy.

So you really didn't see yourself as a candidate for the MVP?

If you look at who's won in the past, it's mostly home run hitters and batters with lots of RBIs. I was sure they wouldn't pick a batter like me, who's first up in the order and gets hits but isn't a home run hitter. Which made it all the more surprising that I won. Afterwards I saw the ballots that the reporters who pick the MVP had written; two reporters from each hometown vote, and for instance one of the Oakland reporters voted for Giambi, Boone, and Thome, but not for me. Thome's a good home run hitter, so that made sense. And actually there were a lot of reporters who voted for the home run hitters. Knowing that made me even happier I'd won. I'd won the most votes even with this set idea that the MVP equals a home run hitter.

What did your wife say at the time?

She was right beside me when I took the call, and congratulated me.

She must have been just as happy as you were at the news.

She's been there to support me, but it hasn't been easy for her. I'm always part of a team, and on the field there are people I can count on to help me out, but living in Seattle she's had to take care of everything all by herself. Emotionally it's been way harder on her than on me, and I know it's been stressful for her. She's really been able to hold up well. I'm always grateful to her that she's been there in the struggle with me.

How did you feel yourself, Yumiko?

Yumiko: I was so happy when I heard he'd won the MVP that I couldn't stop crying. I can't put into words how happy I was.

So, after leaving Japan, Ichiro, you've had to adjust to a completely new environment, but have still been able to concentrate on baseball. And the American people have responded by rooting for you as a major-league player. America's always been the kind of country where people show respect for a challenger.

That's definitely true. I could really feel how America responds positively to anyone—no matter where he's from—who rises to a challenge. At the same time, though, they're pretty hard nosed about wanting to see what kind of stuff the new guy's made of. That's why I knew I had to show them what I was capable of.

As the lead-off hitter, you get on base, use your speed in base running and defense, and use your great arm to pick off runners. The kind of play that made full use of all your talents.

Right. When I said that I wanted to enjoy baseball, deep down one of the things I meant was that I wanted to push the envelope in terms of what I'm capable of doing.

Before you won the MVP, the American media said you'd given America back the excitement in baseball they haven't seen in decades. In the last few years the focus has mainly been on players who can crank out the home runs. That's definitely one of the exciting aspects of baseball, but TV commentators and sportswriters have been saying that it's this Japanese player, Ichiro, who's made them remember the joy found in the kind of baseball that emphasizes hitting, running, and fielding. One reporter even made the comment that you're like the great players of old come back to life. In other words, they're all praising the kind of baseball that uses your entire mental and physical ability, rather than just the kind that counts home runs and RBIs. You get the impression that major-league baseball's changed.

I hadn't really given it a lot of thought, and I was surprised when I heard those kinds of comments from so many fans and people in the media. Personally I've always thought that a baseball player has to be outstanding at all aspects of the game—throwing, catching, hitting, and running. And of course I still believe this after joining the Mariners. I just did what I've always done. But people saw this as something "new" that made baseball exciting again. I was pretty surprised, since I wasn't out there playing trying to get people to say that about me.

In the 2001 season you pushed yourself whenever you were out on the field, giving it everything you had. The fans loved it when you got infield hits or bunted as the leadoff batter. I know you just did your own thing, but it ended up really getting the fans involved, and bringing you the Rookie of the Year award and the MVP. I'd say breaking the mold by winning the MVP is a kind of "major league" achievement in itself.

You have your players who are out there struggling to win, and your fans who get into it. And in the middle of all that to get picked for the MVP is the happiest thing of all for me.

After you won, did the importance of it all sink in?

The MVP also shows that people have high expectations of you. So I was really happy, and at the same time I feel how much more the fans expect of me now. Apart from that, now that I've won it I don't just want to rest on my laurels.

The MVP, in other words, is based on last season and you want to start the new season with a clean slate?

Correct. Whether people rate you high or at the bottom, that's a value judgment from outside of you, not the principle I use to guide myself by. I never want to lose sight of who I really am.

An award, then, is always something you get from a third party.

I'm really happy to receive the award, but I don't want to be influenced by the way some third party feels about me. I've received my fair share of awards during my baseball career and people have asked me how this MVP award would rate. Of course it's the greatest honor I've ever received, but you have to remember that opinions about players change all the time—one moment you're up, the next moment you're down. And I think it's dangerous to let my feelings be swayed by that.

You don't want to lose your own set of values.

Exactly. To give you an example, after I won the award a lot of people said, "Ichiro's fantastic, since he won the MVP." I'm happy I won, but I don't want to be swayed by others' assessment of me. What's most important is to really get my own sense of what I've accomplished. If I don't keep that in mind, somewhere along the line I'll get derailed. Win the MVP and everybody says you're great. Everywhere you go people make a fuss over you. People like to get all worked up; it makes them feel good. But once you get used to that and get carried away by it, you lose a sense of who you really are. The baseball season's pretty long, and you can be sure that if you don't perform you're going to get criticized. If you rely only on the opinions of other people your weaknesses are bound to come out. That's my take on it. So what's vital to me is my own tough, no-nonsense evaluation of how I'm doing. It's very important to be able to examine yourself that way, and if you do that you can stay strong, no matter how people's opinions of you might fluctuate. With the new season coming I especially want to keep that firmly in mind.

Spring Training

After playing in the Cactus League games during your first spring training, you played in your first major league game on April 2, 2001, at Safeco Field, the home ground of the Seattle Mariners. When was it that you really got a sense of what the majors were all about, that you'd become a member of the Mariners team? Did it happen all of a sudden, or little by little the more games you played?

A little of both, actually. There were moments when I suddenly was really aware of the majors, but there were other things it took the whole season to get. The feeling that I was really in the majors came about pretty gradually. Though as far as batting goes, I did have a kind of dramatic moment. A moment when I realized, "Hey, if this is what it's all about then I should be able to get some hits." That might have been the turning point of feeling that I could make it in the majors.

So you made a big step forward in your batting.

A discovery, I'd call it, rather than a big step forward.

You told me before about how in a game against the Seibu Lions in April 1999, when you were facing the pitcher Yukihiro Nishizaki, and you grounded out to second, in that instant you realized how to correct something wrong in your batting. Did you have the same sort of feeling this time about batting?

Yes. Actually, in preseason games in the Peoria spring training camp in March 2001, I did feel worried about hitting in the majors. I stood in the batter's box thinking how different it was from what I was used to, concerned that things weren't going to work out. I didn't think I'd be able to get hits the way I usually did.

There really was a time like that?

I knew if things didn't change I might not become a regular on the Mariner's roster. Because I wasn't able to get to pitches the way I wanted to.

Why is that?

Because I was using the same batting form and timing I'd brought with me from Japan. No matter how many times I went up to bat, nothing worked. I just couldn't get the feeling. At first I encouraged myself, thinking that if I just gave it some time I'd get that feeling back. I'm the type of player who takes a while to get up to speed in the spring. But that old feeling just wouldn't come. I'd studied videos of major-league pitchers and was pretty sure I'd be able to handle them, but I couldn't. The situation got steadily worse and I finally discovered where the problem lay. I realized it was my batting itself that was the problem.

So it wasn't anything to do with the new environment or your physical condition, but your batting itself.

That's right. Things had gotten pretty bad, and while I was trying to figure out the cause I realized that the pitchers in Japan and in the U.S. have different timing when they pitch. Most Japanese pitchers have a pitching form that allows the batter plenty of time. It's like they're going "One, two, and— three," with the "and" part extra long.

Is this a special kind of timing that Japanese pitchers have?

Yes. American pitchers don't have the "and" part in their timing. They just come right at you. And they don't pause a lot between pitches. They don't pick up the rosin bag after each pitch, either. They just come at you bam, bam, bam, which means the batter has to get ready right away.

They say that Japanese pitchers are instructed to pause for a moment to gather their strength together, but what specifically is different?

If you watch American pitchers closely you'll see that there's hardly any pause to get set. Lots of pitchers have a fast tempo— it's just "one, two, three" and go, with no pause. What happened was that my own timing was in sync with timing that had this pause, and that threw my batting off ever so slightly. I knew I had to change my timing if I wanted to get any hits.

Back when you played with Orix in Japan, it was getting your batting in tune with that pause in the setup of Japanese pitchers that led you to develop your unique batting form, which brought you seven batting titles in a row.

In a word, yes, that's right. When I played for Orix I'd lift my right foot in time with that pause in the pitcher's setup. Of course it wasn't easy since I had to get in tune with each pitcher, but I was able to get the timing right while raising my right foot.

In the majors, though, that sort of lifting of the right foot to get the timing right didn't work.

That's right. So I got rid of the timing I used when I played for Orix, and started fresh, with a clean slate, to figure out a new sense of timing. And that's how I could adjust to the major-league pitchers' timing. I was able to get it down right away. And in a flash the strange feeling I'd had in spring training just disappeared.

When was this?

It must have been about the middle of March.

How did you go about getting this new sense of timing?

I dusted off the batting form I had a long time ago. The kind of batting that omitted the special extra pause that Japanese pitchers throw in. This might work, I thought, and it turned out to be perfect. This was the batting form I used before the 1994 season, the 210-hit season. If you look at my form right now it's probably pretty close to the way I batted in '92 and '93 when I was in the Japanese minors.

So the batting form you'd shelved for eight years made a comeback in the majors.

Right. Standing in the batter's box I kept thinking something's wrong here, and I couldn't figure out what to do. So finally one day I decided to try the way I used to bat, without lifting my right leg. This was while we were playing these pre-season games, and I stood in front of the mirror at the Peoria stadium and, without holding a bat, practiced over and over so I could get a mental image of it. That's how I started to get this new timing down.

You knew you had it then.

I checked it out in practice, and in each game we played, and things started to click. Every time I swung the bat I felt I'd found it.

I have noticed a definite change in your batting form from before you joined the majors—the way you don't lift your right foot anymore. So that's your major-league batting style?

Right. All the basics are still the same, though. It isn't like I've changed from tracking the ball as a line to seeing it as a point or anything. I still try to bring the bat so it strikes the track of the ball that I've picked up visually. Just the timing has changed.

Does it feel like you're moving faster?

It's not faster, it's omitting a part. I time things without that pause the pitcher might add. Compared to Japanese pitchers there's less excess movement in major-league pitchers' form, so I've got to cut out the excess myself so I can stay in tune with them.

So your timing was now perfect for pitchers who omit that extra pause in their delivery. But if a batter omits that moment, that pause, doesn't it mean you can't get set yourself? In theory, batters, too, need that pause to gather their strength, not just to blast the ball as far as they can, but to get some good wood on the ball, right? Major-league pitchers throw the ball faster and with more on it than Japanese pitchers, and if you omit getting set up when you want to make good contact you might end up on the short end of the stick.

Omitting that pause and getting set up are two different things. Before, I used to get all set by raising my right foot, but I can still get completely set without doing that. In 2000, my last season in Japan, I'm pretty sure I kept my right foot down much more than before. And now I keep it even closer to the ground. The movement of my right foot, and the lower half of my body, have become more compact. But this process of getting set isn't done by raising the right leg, but by what the batter does with his left leg, the inner part of your left leg. It takes place in your adductor muscles, and the inner part of your knee. Getting set isn't necessarily linked to raising your right foot. You can get set without raising your right foot at all.

You can get completely set by the way you use the rest of your body, then.

Right. And what I did with my left leg, the one that you need to get set, didn't change at all.

So even without raising your right foot this doesn't negatively impact the amount of power you can get at the moment of impact.

Not at all. If you know how to concentrate your power and get set with your left leg then the right foot is irrelevant.

I find it fascinating, though, that when you had just become a

*pro you found you couldn't consistently hit with the kind of bat-
ting you'd been doing up till then, which led to this form where you
raise your right foot, and then your batting average went up. But
now what's saved you in the majors is the batting form you'd dis-
carded in Japan.*

I thought I'd never need to use that older batting form again.
Lifting my right foot like that let me hit the way I wanted, so I
thought there wasn't any need. But in the majors I found I
needed to resurrect the old technique. Discovering this and
finding a solution to my problem was definitely a turning
point for me as I was starting out in the majors.

*By the end of spring training, then, you'd gotten rid of any
doubts you had about your batting.*

Yeah, I thought this would work. I'd gotten the timing down,
so things should go OK. That's when I really started batting.

Did you have any concerns as the season started?

Sure I did, but I was confident I could make it.

Building a Wall and Pulling the Ball

*In the beginning American sportswriters and reporters were say-
ing, "This Ichiro Suzuki hits everything to left field. Why doesn't
he hit to the right?" Apparently it was a hot topic of conversation.
Lou Piniella, your manager, also seemed concerned that you were
hitting everything to the opposite field and not pulling any pitches.
And it does seem true that in the early stages you were hitting
everything to left. After a certain point when you started hitting*

to right as well, Piniella told reporters, laughing, "That's what I've been waiting to see. If he could hit to right all this time I want to tell him, 'Hey, why did you wait till now to show me that?'" Was there some reason you were hitting like that? Is there a connection between this and omitting a motion to get your timing right?

It has nothing to do with omitting something to adjust the timing. This is a little complicated, but first of all it has to do with the strike zone. The major-league strike zone, compared to Japan's, is much wider on the outside. I had to get used to this. Inside pitches, if they're over the plate, are strikes, but, different from Japan, if they miss one balls' width on the inside they're seldom called a strike. I'm not saying they never are, but compared to pitches on the outside of the plate, they're much less often called strikes.

If the pitch is on the outside of the plate, one ball width outside, it's often called a strike, right?

That's right. All of which means I have to be much more aware of outside pitches than when I was playing in Japan. In reality, as I stand in the batter's box I have to somehow handle inside pitches while also paying attention to ones on the outside of the plate. But it's really hard to pay attention to inside pitches and pick up pitches that are one or two balls' width outside. Which means I have to focus my concentration on the outside of the plate, where it's easy to get called on strikes. As I track the ball, my focus has to be on the area from the middle of the plate to the outside corner. And then if you hit those pitches on the outside they're naturally going to go to left.

Focusing on outside pitches and then pulling them to right is really tough.

So your hits to the opposite field, then, were your way of dealing with the strike zone that's wider to the outside.

Yes. And even the pitches inside I would tend to hit with a sort of inside-out swing, which would make most of them go to left. But there's another reason for this besides the strike zone.

Which is?

As I start a new season, with a long series of games ahead of me, there's a process I go through in order to get my batting up to speed. It's critical to create what I call a "wall" on the right side of my body. This process is important for batters, the thing we struggle with the most. And creating this wall is one of the things you have to do at the beginning of spring. It's something I did all the time I was playing in Japan.

When you say a "wall," what exactly do you mean?

It's the process of getting your batting form set. For a left-handed batter like myself, as I set up facing the pitcher I create the mental image of a large wall on the surface of the right side. Once I get this invisible wall all set my batting form is solid and I'm able to hit to left, to center, and to right. In order to strengthen this wall in the beginning I have to be more conscious of the area left of center. Not that I couldn't pull a ball to the right all of a sudden, but if I do that my form breaks down. The reason my hits in the beginning of the spring were mostly left of center—and the same was true when I was in Japan—is because I was still in the process of constructing that wall. I like to wait until the wall is all set before I pull balls to right. I have to do that to make it through the season without my batting form breaking down.

Is this your own unique concept, the idea of a wall on your right side as you face the pitcher?

I think all batters must have the same concept. All batters think about the process of getting their form solidified.

So while you were building this "wall" in spring training you hit everything left of center, which worried your manager. Did you tell him and the coaches the reason for this?

I don't talk much about myself, because it sounds like I'm trying to make excuses. Especially something like this "creating a wall" process, which is entirely an internal thing, is pretty hard to convey to somebody else so they truly understand it. It's better not to say something if you don't know how it's going to be taken; in this case actions speak louder than words.

I guess it could be hard to explain a complicated technical process like that.

It's more convincing for people to see the process and the progress you make.

A few days after Piniella started worrying about this you started to hit to right field and he reportedly said, "There's nothing more I need to say to Ichiro." So when you started hitting to right that meant your "wall" was all complete.

I guess he really was worried after all. The people who hire you want to see results, and it's only natural they want to see everything you're capable of. It's reasonable he'd expect this.

The sort of balance you have to maintain in a situation like that is pretty delicate, though. You want to kind of unobtrusively go about your business, dealing with issues you need to tackle, but you also need to give the manager and coaches, not to mention your teammates, the confidence that you can handle your assignment. The ideal, I think, is to show them through what you accomplish on the field that you can handle it, even if you don't talk about it much.

Major-League Debut

Finally on April 2 you played your first game at Safeco Field. Right from the start of the season you didn't let the team down in your role as leadoff batter. You piled up the hits, thanks to which the team was on a roll.

That was my one major assignment—getting things started as the leadoff batter. To get on base and put some pressure on the opposing battery. That's the most effective way to grab the initiative in a game.

I've heard that players in the majors don't practice nearly as much before games compared to Japan. Is that true?

It's true, they don't.

Did that feel strange to you?

In Japan I asked my coaches to let me prepare for the game at my own pace. So I didn't do as much practice as the other players do. But here they don't even practice shagging fungoes at each position. It's important just before a game to get focused, and even when I was in Japan I always wanted to practice that if possible just before a game, but here we've never done it—not even once. The total amount of time we have to get ready is pretty short, so it's really important to get yourself prepared for the game, otherwise you run the risk of getting injured. If we have a night game followed by a day game the next day, we don't do any practice together as a team. We don't run, we don't do any stretching, just some light batting practice in the batting cage. The rest is up to each individual player. I like to warm up by running up and down the hallway in front of the locker room. In most ballparks the batting cage is out in the middle, right below the stands, and before I go out to batting practice I always run down the corridor that leads to there.

The Mariners got off to a good start as the season got under way. And I think they started to put a lot of faith in you as the leadoff batter pretty early on, didn't they?

I'm not sure about that [when they started to put their trust in me], but I think it took longer than the month of April. There are some players who basically perform well only in the beginning of the season. That's why there were all sorts of views about my performance among the Mariners players then, not just positive opinions.

There really were negative views from people who wondered whether you'd be able to cut it?

If I said there wasn't concern among the team, I wouldn't be telling the truth.

Well, after all, you were the first Japanese position player to play in the majors, so I suppose it's only natural that some people wondered whether you'd be able to really help out the team.

I think that's right. Performance on the field is always the number-one priority, but if you want to be a member of the team other intangible factors, too, are important—respect, friendship, etc. Even things like your attitude and facial expression matter.

On April 6 in a game in Texas against the Rangers, not long after the season opened, you hit your first home run. After the game you said, "Let's just say I wasn't trying to hit one," but it really looked like you were trying to hit one out of there.

Of course I was trying to hit it. Almost 100 percent of my home runs are ones where I'm aiming to hit a home run. Our batting coach, Gerald Perry, gets upset when I try to hit homers during practice. I think he must figure that because I'm on the small side for a major-league player it's better not to try to hit home runs.

Do the manager and coaching staff try to convince you of the role you're supposed to play, and try to get you to follow their theories on how to go about it?

There really isn't a lot of that.

When you hit that home run, what was the reaction of the coaching staff and your teammates?

Hmm—I think everybody thought it was just a fluke. That had to be what they were thinking, the way they carried on when I hit it.

During April you went on a hitting streak and set a new hitting record for Mariner rookies. This was the first time you'd experienced the majors every day, but the fans must have been pretty thrilled by your hitting streak. Just as in Japan, expectations started to build for you to get more and more hits. Did you feel much pressure?

The atmosphere of the stadium is different, and there's the problem of communicating in English. The stadiums were new to me, too, and I did feel a bit tense. But I was able to enjoy playing. I was able to adjust my form the way I wanted to, and that "wall" I was talking about was all set, so I didn't feel any anxiety. I hit in fifteen straight games after my first hit. When that happened people started to react like, Hey this new guy's not bad. After that I didn't hit in one game, then got a hit in twenty-three straight games, and I think people's opinions about me gradually began to change.

Whenever you got on base that seemed to get the team going. You're able to beat out a lot of infield grounders and get on base, and your speed on the bases put a lot of pressure on your opponents. You'd get a hit as the leadoff batter and that seemed to be the pattern as the Mariners became nearly unstoppable.

I might get a hit and get on base, but if the other players up after me don't make something happen we're not going to win. No matter how much your leadoff guy gets on base, what's really important is figuring out how to get him home. That's part of how I'll be evaluated. The other players make something happen for me, and that means I make something happen for them. That's what it means for the team to be in sync.

When it looked like you were going to steal that always put a lot of pressure on the battery and you could tell it got to pitchers and made them jumpy.

I like it when I'm showing the pitcher I might take off at any minute and it makes him a little edgy.

Did you get faster running to first on a hit and stealing bases than when you played for Orix?

I don't think it's possible to become faster than the year before. When I played for Orix I didn't hold back on running at all. In the last few seasons in Japan I batted third or fourth, and, compared to that, batting leadoff for the Mariners made me much more aware of running. People are all expecting something of my base running now, I think. And I have the same heightened sense of expectation.

They say you can run to first in 3.6 seconds.

I'm not sure if that's true or not.

But you definitely look faster.

The way I bat has a lot to do with that. I make a major weight shift when I swing, and it's critical to get a smooth first step toward first. To the players here, apparently it looks like I'm already running before I hit the ball. I try my best to start running only after I've completed my swing, but they tell me I'm hitting and running at the same time. It's strange, because I don't think that's what I'm doing at all.

When they say that—that you're hitting the ball while you're running—it's not some throwaway remark, but something that tries to express how very revolutionary your batting is compared to other players'. *Even major-league players can't understand your batting. In both America and Japan the basic theory of batting is to keep your weight on the foot closest to the catcher when you hit the ball, but in your case at the moment of impact you shift your weight onto your right foot, the foot nearer the pitcher, away from your left foot. You're not starting to run, but since it's an unusual style of batting maybe it looks to other people not that you're shifting your weight but that you are actually starting to run. It's critical that the leadoff batter get on base. If you shift your weight from your left foot to your right as part of your swing, a series of movements begins that gets you started off toward first base, which definitely gives you an advantage.*

That might be the case. Certainly the shift of weight and running are linked. But actually there are other players who do the same sort of weight shift. You can see this really well in batting practice, where the Mariners' designated hitter, Edgar Martinez, does this. He bats right-handed, and in theory he shouldn't move his right leg, his pivot point, but he moves it a lot. Among the Mariners players I've found his batting the most useful to study.

You study his batting?

I watch him in games, of course, but also in practice. It's helped me a lot.

The other big guns for the Mariners—Bret Boone and John Olerud—bat very differently from you, don't they? Olerud's joked that he won't allow his kids to imitate Ichiro's batting style.

I'd probably say the same thing.

Your batting style's begun to have an influence on children, though. Apparently there are lots of Little Leaguers who imitate you. Kids think it's cool not just to hit home runs now, but to run as fast as they can to get a hit. I saw on the news how you visited an elementary school once, and the way they cheered you was deafening. You could see on the kids' faces how happy they were to have their hero visit.

It's a very nice thing when your performance on the field gets noticed like that. Fans who enjoy major-league baseball want to see all sorts of exciting plays. Nothing could make me happier than to be able to add something new and exciting. But I never imagined that my style of play would get such a reaction. With so many outstanding players coming up one after another in the majors, I thought I'd just be categorized as a certain type of player and that would be that. It's wonderful that people can recognize and enjoy my individual style.

Your batting was truly amazing. On June 10 you got your 100th hit faster than anybody else [later, one of Ichiro's previous hits was eventually ruled an error, making his next hit in the following game the 100th], and people started to say, "This guy Ichiro won the batting crown seven times in a row in Japan, so how can you call him a rookie?" Were you starting to sense the impact you were having?

It wasn't like I was always thinking, "Hey, I'm really getting some results here in the majors." Though as things took their course I did start to get more relaxed. Major-league pitchers have incredible fight in them and never back away from a batter. Even if they're not pitching well they gut it out. If I couldn't stand up to those kind of tough pitchers in other words, if I were even just a little unsure of myself I wouldn't have gotten the results I wanted. When you're facing pitchers that are that confident in their ability, if you don't have your own technique and aren't strong emotionally, the hits just aren't going to come.

The media and the fans got all worked up over you, but you yourself weren't all that excited.

I was excited. But I wasn't as surprised by it as the people watching me.

You were just keeping a level head and showing what you could do.

Exactly.

In '94, when you got 210 hits in Japan, you said you felt you'd been given something beyond your own power, but this past season was something quite different, wasn't it?

Yes, it was different.

From April to June the Mariners had two stretches of thirteen straight games, plus a hard schedule that took you to lots of different cities for games.

It wasn't easy, but it's all relative. It did seem easier than traveling to away games in Japan, though. With the Mariners, after we'd play a series of away games we'd always travel right away to the next city, even if it meant starting after midnight, and that helped me out a lot. I'm not a morning person, and find it hard to travel the next morning, which we never did. Also it was much less stressful because we didn't see anybody else until we got to the hotel. Traveling to the next city in Japan is tough. You're on the bullet train trying to catch a few winks and people are often waking you up to get your autograph. That's really hard on you. In America, though, even if it takes five hours to get to where we're going, it's just members of the team in the plane so you can sleep uninterrupted. It's definitely less stressful.

Does the team have the plane all to itself?

Yes, we charter planes. There are two types of charters, depending on how far we're going. If it's far away we take a larger plane and each of us has three seats in economy class so we can lie down and sleep. When we take smaller planes we sit in business-class seats and we can't lie down, but it's still comfortable. Whenever we traveled I just slept.

On the road you had to deal with time-zone changes and different climates depending on the place, didn't you?

Playing against the Devil Rays in Tampa, Florida, was pretty tough. Tampa's the farthest city away from Seattle we played in, plus with the time difference I couldn't sleep much for a few days and played three games in a row on two or three hours' sleep a night. The final game of the series in Tampa started at noon, I believe, but with the time difference that would be 9 A.M. Seattle time. The three-hour time difference was hard on me. Kansas City and Texas were hot, sometimes getting up to more than 100 degrees. But the most we'd be in any place was four days, so I could always manage to tough it out.

Were you able to stay in shape even with staying in hotels all the time?

As long as I slept and ate enough that wasn't a problem.

Where did you eat?

Never in the hotel. Often we'd get restaurants to open up especially for us late at night. That helped me a lot. It's still not easy going out to eat.

I understand you like Japanese food best. Seattle and Los Angeles have Japanese restaurants, but in some cities it must be hard to find any.

Yeah, it's not like in Japan.

Are you able to sleep well in hotels?

The room has to be pitch dark or else I can't get to sleep. Some hotels just have blinds but no curtains. The light gets in and it irritates me and I can't sleep. I realize that's going to happen sometimes. But overall being on the road isn't as hard as in Japan.

The All-Star Game

In the middle of the season came the news that you'd been picked for the All-Star Game. In the past you said that you couldn't imagine playing in the MLB (Major League Baseball) All-Star Game, but if by chance you were selected it'd be a lot to live up to. When the time came that you actually played in the All-Star Game did you feel how heavy that responsibility was?

I was selected for the All-Stars by vote of the fans, and I received more than three million votes. That's pressure, pure and simple, I can tell you—pressure to live up to the expectations those votes represent. As soon as people started talking about the All-Stars they said I've got to be one of the players picked. It's the same thing with the MVP, but when you're selected for the All-Stars you can't just rest on your laurels. It's like you can't be satisfied at where you're at now, like you've been given the impetus to take your game to the next level.

Just before the game you said you were the one who was looking forward to it the most, but you still felt more pressure than you ever imagined.

I loved playing in that game. Pressure is something I have to deal with as long as I play baseball. I feel it even now. And it is heavy.

I wonder if you would comment on going up against Randy Johnson. He used to be a Mariner, with the same number, 51.

Curt Shilling was originally scheduled as the starter, but I had a feeling they'd change to Randy Johnson. Just looking at the pitching rotation schedule of their team [the Arizona Diamondbacks], I thought they wouldn't start Schilling in the All-Star Game. Of course when it all came about I thought, "Now we're in for it."

Randy Johnson stands six feet ten inches. You'd never see pitchers in Japan throwing from that height, and his 100-miles-per-hour-plus fastball isn't all that common even in America, is it?

I agree. Randy seems much closer to you than other pitchers. And he comes at you from the side, a combination that makes him definitely not an easy pitcher to face.

You really smacked the second pitch, though. A bullet down the first baseline. Normally that would have gone through for extra bases, but the first basemen, Todd Helton [of the Colorado Rockies] made a fine play. Otherwise it might have been a double, even a triple.

Now that I think of it, I think that was the only day [the whole season] I could swing the bat without worrying about the outcome of the game.

The crowd loves that one-on-one showdown, too.

Every time I looked around during the game I got that feeling of "Wow! These are the All-Stars."

So at the All-Star Game the players have a good time?

I think so, but everyone's also pretty serious about it. It doesn't count in the pennant race, but your pride is a factor.

The home run that Cal Ripken, Jr., who retired last season, hit was like something out of a drama.

It really was. But the pitcher who gave up the homer—Chan Ho Park—wasn't laughing. Batters smiled when they got hits, but not when they struck out. It's fun to play in an All-Star Game, all right, but everyone feels the responsibility of being selected and you know your honor and pride are on the line.

The competition was pretty fierce, and you could sense how thick the tension was. Another memorable event in the game was the ceremony they had in the sixth inning to honor Ripken and Tony Gwynn, who were both retiring. America is really the best in the world at putting on those kind of events.

Absolutely. I had already come out of the game and been replaced by another player, so I'd gone to the locker room. Ivan

Rodriguez came in and said there was going to be a ceremony and I'd better come back out to be a part of it. Everybody was running out on the field to join in, so I had to run like crazy to catch up.

Yumiko, where did you watch the All-Star Game?

Yumiko: In the stands. The game was going to be played in Seattle so I definitely wanted to see it, and we got tickets for the two of us.

So, Ichiro, you were planning to enjoy the game from the stands?

Yeah, that's right. Have a hot dog, sit back, and enjoy watching the All-Star Game being played right on my home field—that was the plan. Being selected to play in the All-Star Game just came totally out of the blue. It was like something from a movie, it was so surprising—the All-Star Game being played in Seattle and me being a part of it. And then having the starting pitcher suddenly change from Curt Schilling to Randy Johnson, the guy who wore number 51 in Seattle before me, and batting against him. Something's definitely going on here, is how it felt to me.

A Dry Spell

After the All-Star Game the season resumed, and you went hitless for four straight games and people started to whisper about you being in a slump. What was the situation at that time?

It all depends on your definition of slump. If by slump you mean not getting any hits, then that was definitely a slump. But there are also times when you don't get any hits but you still have the sense that you can get a hit. If you define a slump as when you've lost the feeling, your batting sense, then that wasn't a slump I was in. Even when I wasn't getting any hits I hadn't lost that sense at all.

So there were times at bat when you felt you could get a hit?

There were. I was able to track the ball well. I went hitless for twenty times at bat, but twelve out of the twenty I felt I could have gotten a hit. My timing was off ever so slightly and I mishit the ball. I didn't feel anxious about it or anything, because there wasn't anything wrong with my batting.

You weren't afraid that if things continued like that you wouldn't be able to get a hit?

No, not at all. Though the longer I went hitless, the more pressure I felt from those around me. I heard them talk about me being in a slump. Then you start to step into the batter's box with the weight of all those previous at bats on your shoulders. Like say you've gone hitless ten times, and when you're at bat the eleventh time you have to have all eleven at bats on your shoulders at once. And that mental aspect might very well end up throwing off the overall motion you have that gives you the sense that you can hit. And it's true that sort of thing built up. At the time I really wanted even one hit.

On July 17 against the Diamondbacks you finally got a hit, and I imagine you breathed a sigh of relief?

It was more a sense of relief that everyone around me could relax now.

On August 6 you set a new record for rookies with the Mariners, getting your 161st hit, and on the 28th you reached 200 hits faster than anyone else in either league. You were cranking out the hits. Was getting your 200th hit in the majors especially meaningful for you?

Hmm.... Reaching 200 is a major goal. As you go about your business of hitting, it's the one number you probably see as a tangible goal. Batting averages fluctuate, so I don't set a goal for that. But I guess for a batter 200 hits is a sort of barrier. And in the majors, too, I was conscious of that [of 200 hits].

There are more games in one season in the majors than in Japan, so is the meaning of 200 hits a little different?

It is. In the 130- or 135-game season in Japan it's a hard number to reach. [Ichiro set a new Japanese record in 1994 with 210 hits. At that time, the season was 130 games.] With the longer season in the majors you do have a few players who reach that figure. So you can't think of it in the same way as in Japan. In 2001 the season in Japan was expanded to 140 games, though, which should mean more players reaching 200 hits.

When you joined the majors were you thinking about getting 200 hits?

I started to think about it when I had only a few hits left to go to reach that number. The first time I got a hit it wasn't something I was thinking about. But as I approached 200 that number did become a goal.

As you got closer to 200 the Japanese and American media coverage started to get pretty intense. Did it bother you?

I never read or listen to any news reports about me. I know what's going on with the reporters around me, but people from the Japanese media sympathized with my desire to concentrate on what I was doing. I'm very grateful to them for doing that.

9.11 Shock and Clinching the Division Title

As September rolled around it was pretty clear that the Mariners would win the Western Division of the American League. But with the terrorist attacks of September 11, all major-league games were stopped, something that hasn't happened since World War I. You were playing in Anaheim at the time, and what was the situation like there?

The game that day was canceled, as was the next day's game, which was the final game of the series. All I could do was rest back at the hotel, since there was no way to get back to Seattle. No planes were flying out of Los Angeles, so they decided to take us by bus to Sacramento. But everything was so confused we didn't know if there'd be any planes flying out of Sacramento or not. In the end we found out we'd be able to leave from L.A. in a few days, so we flew back to Seattle from there.

Where were you, Yumiko?

Yumiko: That's one of the trips a lot of the wives went on because they were likely to clinch the division title during that series, so I happened to be there, too.

I would have worried if we hadn't been together. It was a relief we were together. Our magic number for clinching the division title was two, but the team was resigned to the season ending right then and there. For the rest of my life I'll remember the shock I felt when I saw the World Trade Center on TV.

A week later, on September 18, the pennant race resumed. You had to play in the midst of these shattering events that had happened.

To me, that game a week after the attack wasn't even like a game in the pennant race. It meant something far more significant: that baseball had returned to America. It went way beyond winning and losing.

On September 19 the Mariners clinched their third division title, the first in four years. All the players had American flags on their uniforms, and after you won some of the players prayed silently under the flag that Mark McLemore held up. That scene makes you realize how much baseball means to the American people. I imagine you had a lot of feelings about this, too.

Each person has his role to play. At that time we were wondering what we could do. Baseball players are public figures, after all. And we have a real responsibility. The thought did cross my mind that maybe it wasn't a good idea to reopen the season, but once I stood on the field again I understood how much Americans had been waiting for this game. It struck me that this was precisely the time when the game must go on.

The Mariners won the division title with a tremendous record of 116 wins. What's your take on why the team was so strong and able to win so much?

It's a record that we never would have reached without the abilities of each and every player. I think it was because all the potential that the players had was added into the equation. Also, early on we established a pattern for our wins. As long as our starting pitcher could make it to the fifth or sixth inning, we could then leave it in the hands of our bullpen. So if we were at least one run up we knew there was a good chance we could win. To pull off the win each player had to concentrate on what he could do to get the job done. For me that meant getting on base and scoring. What we did was pretty simple, I think.

The Mariners seemed to have an emotional toughness about them, too.

Once we got on a roll, it was like we couldn't allow ourselves to lose. No one ever wanted to give up. We were a determined group of players. If I gave up even a little, it would have been obvious—I would have stood out. That's the kind of team we are.

There was an amazing strength there.

Which is why we were able to end up with 116 wins and only 46 losses.

There was a different flow to Mariners games compared to when Ken Griffey, Jr., and Alex Rodriguez were on the team. You'd play to get someone on base and then do whatever it took to bring him home. This kind of baseball that doesn't rely on home run hitters is really exciting.

We have a lot of versatile players. For instance, Mark McLemore, who we relied on to play so many different positions, would suddenly be put in left field and make a great play there. Guys were able to move around in the batting order and perform wherever they were put. In fact, I was the only batter who was never shifted to a different position in the batting order the entire season. Every time they put a player in a different position or mixed up the batting order, guys did exactly what they were called on to do. Our team was that talented. Usually, when the batting order changes frequently, players grumble and their rhythms get disrupted, but our guys did whatever was asked and never complained.

How do they decide the starting lineup and the batting order?

It's posted in the locker room on the day of the game.

So Lou Piniella, the manager, would decide that based on the players' condition and who you were playing against that day?

That's right. And it makes the players want to do the best they can. Out on the field it was clear he left things up to the players.

Not too long ago Piniella had such a temper they called him a real hothead.

I think he chews gum to keep a lid on it. He's never once yelled at me in the dugout, though when I'm in the batter's box he always says something.

He is somewhat uncompromising.

That's exactly right. Looking back on this first season in the majors I realized that, say, in a game where I'd already gotten two hits, that doesn't mean that the third time up he's going to cut me some slack. I might have batted in a run the last time up, but that doesn't mean at all that grounding out the next time up is going to be overlooked. It's a tough, uncompromising stance.

Passing Shoeless Joe

And in the midst of that uncompromising approach you set several records. On September 29 you broke the rookie hits record by reaching 233 hits. Breaking the record by the legendary Shoeless Joe Jackson that had stood for ninety years.

I'd heard about his hitting record, and naturally [the number] stuck in my mind. That put pressure on me, but I was really happy I could break that record—it was a great feeling.

It really gives you a sense of major league history, doesn't it—that the record you were trying to break was set 90 years ago by Shoeless Joe.

Major-league fans are really knowledgeable about players of the past and records. The history of the game is important to them. I don't know about these at all, though I do understand how much weight tradition has in the majors.

On October 7 when the pennant race was over, you were both the top batter and top base stealer. You'd left behind a brilliant season, with a .350 batting average and fifty-six stolen bases. How did you feel about ending up the top batter?

In the middle of the season, when I was in the top three in batting average, I looked at it pretty dispassionately, wondering who was going to come out on top. That's probably because I was pretty sure it wasn't going to be me. I'm not sure why I felt that way. I was always wondering at which point my name would disappear from the list of top batters. As we played more games, though, my average didn't go up all that much, but the other top batters dropped their average and I just sort of emerged. Still, though, it wasn't like I was hoping I'd get the top spot. Again I'm not sure why I felt like that. Probably because I was sure that with the competition I had in the end I wasn't going to come out on top. Also near the end of the season Jason Giambi of the Oakland Athletics made a push for it. There are some great players out there, but I never felt attached to winning the title or as if I had to be the top batter. From past experience I know that if I start to really want a title I get too self-conscious and my body gets out of sync. That's what it means when they say the things you want elude you. Maybe that's why I'd developed the habit of not thinking about it [of not considering winning the title].

Unconsciously you shut out those thoughts.

Yes, that's probably true. Or maybe it just didn't hit me at all. I'm still not sure. Anyway, I'm glad I didn't think about wanting to be the top batter. If I'd thought I've got to have this with five or so games left, most likely I'd have gone hitless.

Once you start figuring out batting averages you start to worry about the competition, don't you. Maybe inside you're hoping other players don't get a hit.

Right. If you start wanting it too much you get too concerned about other people. The one thing I can't stand is hoping that other people mess up.

So when did you really think you could get the batting title?

At the very end, when we had maybe one or two games left.

How about the moment you actually won the batting title?

40

That was fantastic.

It must have been a real confidence booster to you to get through the long season so successfully, and end up the top batter.

I never stopped wanting to step up to the plate. I always knew that feeling was going to be a major boost to me. No matter how well Giambi hit, I never felt like backing down. That [feeling inside me] is something that'll keep me going for the rest of my career.

How about base stealing? Because of the difference in number of total games between the U.S. and Japan, again it's hard to make comparisons, but still this was your best total ever, bettering your previous record of forty-nine in 1995. Before the season began you said you hoped to be able to steal as many bases as possible, so was this a record you were aiming at?

Yes, of course. The thing is, the rules about base stealing are different in the two countries, the U.S. and Japan. In the majors, if your team is leading and basically the outcome is obvious, and the first baseman isn't holding you on first and you steal second, it doesn't count in the record books as a steal. That really surprised me to hear that. I had no idea. In the majors they don't let you steal just to run up the numbers. Which means those kinds of steals aren't included in the fifty-six I had for the season. They do this so people won't steal just to pad their stats. I was really impressed by that. The same rules apply to bunting.

To bunting?

Yeah. Let's say there's one out, a runner on second, and you bunt. Even if you get the runner to third it doesn't count as a

A "laser-beam" throw from right field.

sacrifice bunt. In Japan that would count as a sacrifice bunt so your number of at bats wouldn't change, and of course it wouldn't lower your batting average. Here, though, it counts as grounding out, it counts as an at bat, and your average goes down. Bunting negatively impacts your average. Of course there might be some variation, depending on the official scorers. If the runner on second is the pitcher, less or the batter is the pitcher, it might count as a sacrifice bunt. I haven't heard all the details on that one.

Even you weren't aware of these rules, then.

I didn't know. It blew me away to find out the rules weren't the same.

How did you find out about them?

That sort of situation came up in spring training. One out, runner on second. I bunted and was called out at first. The runner advanced to third. But it didn't count as a sacrifice bunt. So I asked them why, and they explained the rule to me.

These are official rules you're talking about, but I understand that in the majors there are also what are called "unwritten rules" of conduct. For example, in a one-sided game when the count's three balls, no strikes, you're not supposed to go after the next pitch, or when you hit a home run you're not supposed to show off by gesturing wildly or taking your time to circle the bases. When Tsuyoshi Shinjo was with the New York Mets last year he hit a home run once and touched home plate with his hand, which apparently is something you're not supposed to do. As payback, maybe, the other team later hit him with a pitch.

Did that really happen? In Japan that wouldn't have been a problem. I feel a little sorry for him.

I remember how they officially overturned a hit you got once. An infield hit was turned into an error by the other team. Several months after the actual game.

Yes, that's right, I remember that. I was really surprised to hear they'd taken a hit away from me. And several months after it happened, too. I remember looking in the newspaper and thinking, wait a second, my total number of hits has gone down by one. That was a surprise. But I've seen a lot of games where the opposite happens, where in a later inning an error is changed into a hit.

The Postseason

Soon after all this the postseason games began. Somehow, though, the Mariners didn't seem to have their A game.

It was like after winning the AL West championship we then got off track.

You were all aware of how important those games were, though, right?

Of course we were. There's a lot of pressure knowing it'll all be over in five games.

There's also the pressure of trying to get into the World Series, I imagine.

And also the pressure that comes from winning so much in the regular season. But our team unity, the sense that we had to get the job done, wasn't affected.

In the division series against the Cleveland Indians you batted .600.

I was able to stay completely calm through the whole thing.

How were you able to do that?

I was tense inside, though I might not have looked like it, but during seven years in Japan I'd put all kinds of pressure on myself. Even at times when I didn't want to feel pressure it was put on me. I'd overcome a lot, which gave me confidence. That experience was very important. No matter what kind of situation came up, no matter what happened, I was able to handle it last season without getting flustered.

Nothing ever fazed you.

Most of the time.

In the series against the Indians you came back to win three games to two. Then you took on the New York Yankees for the AL pennant. You lost in five games, but after the pennant race was over you said that instead of thinking of the Yankees as a strong team or whatever, the Mariners were conscious of the Yankees as the kind of team that always gave you the feeling that something was going to happen. What did you mean by that?

It's something I felt through the whole season. No matter how good our record might be against them, there's a sense of awe that's always there with the Yankees. The atmosphere's different.

For example?

. . . I'm not really sure.

You don't feel that kind of atmosphere with any other team?
Well, all I can say is it's something special.

Looking back on the postseason play, how does it feel that you were just one step away from the World Series?

It was more than just one step. We were still far from it. The Yankees had gone on to the Series four years in a row, and I think they're amazing.

Major-League Pitchers

I'd like to ask you about the pitchers you faced. You faced Pedro Martinez for the first time since the '96 Japan–U.S. All-Star series. He's a true major-league pitcher, I'd say, and what was it like facing him for the first time in a while?

I didn't face him so many times so it's hard to draw any conclusions, but he's throwing more different types of pitches now. Different pitches, plus he's refined the ones he already had. At any rate, he's got all the skills a pitcher needs. Everything you'd imagine a great pitcher has to have. And he's really smart. He makes major adjustments according to the batters he's facing. He can easily change his pace without losing control or making mispitches.

He makes these adjustments based on each batter's personality and weak points?

That's right. He doesn't just think, OK, here's what I've got, and come at you, but controls things by figuring out his opponent's state of mind.

He's a pitcher who stresses the mental aspects of the game.

Exactly.

After the game, Martinez said that you're the only one he couldn't strike out, and seemed a bit frustrated by that.

If a pitcher like that gives you everything he has and you can still hang in there, that's what really makes me happy.

Next is Roger Clemens, the Yankees' ace, and a five-time Cy Young recipient. Poster boy for the major leagues, you might say.

He's different from Pedro. He's the type of dauntless pitcher who keeps coming at you with everything he's got no matter who he's facing. Instead of changing according to the batter he's facing, he's much more the type who sticks to his own style. Each pitch is fantastic; he puts everything into them, which makes him a really tough pitcher to hit.

He's thirty-nine, a very self-controlled person who isn't bothered at all by the most grueling training. He doesn't let his age hold him back at all.

Absolutely. There are a lot of major-league players in their late thirties who are still very active. Even lots of top-ranked pitchers, too. Clemens, Randy Johnson, Greg Maddox.

When you play against them, do you imagine yourself ten years down the line?

Not yet. I won't know what that's like until I actually get to that age. I'm really curious, though, to see what I'll be when I'm, say, thirty-eight.

How about your impression of Troy Percival of the Anaheim Angels and his 100-miles-per-hour fastball?

It has a lot of break in it, very different from your usual major league fastball. A pitch that comes at you straight in, but has a lot of break in it, a lot of spin and sail to it. There are a lot of pitchers who can throw a ball 95, 96 miles per hour, but not many who can throw one with that kind of pure rotation on it. Simply amazing pitches.

How about Steve Sparks [formerly of the Detroit Tigers], who came at you with thirteen knuckleballs out of seventeen pitches? Those kind of knuckleballs are pretty unrelenting, aren't they?

They have a lot of movement on them. They sway so much. It's really frustrating to get out on those kinds of pitches. It makes you feel so dumb, and you get so upset at yourself. And the more upset you get, the less you're able to hit them. And the more that happens, the more things get broken back in the dugout.

They say Sparks changes his pitching form just when he faces you.

It did seem that each time I came up to bat he made some sort of adjustments.

The first time you were hit by a pitch was by one thrown by Hideo Nomo of the Boston Red Sox.

Yeah, I got the wind knocked out of me. By the way, Nomo's no-hit, no-run game was pretty impressive.

Running and Throwing

Your batting average is not the only thing we should note about your batting. One amazing thing is how few times you struck out. Last season you struck out only fifty-three times—one-third the number of times Alex Rodriguez did. Just before the season began you said you wanted to foul off risky pitches and wait for the pitch you wanted to hit. Is that connected with why you struck out so seldom?

Maybe, but the opposite might be true as well. I didn't swing and miss at balls that were right on the borderline between being strikes or foul balls, and the times I struck out there were lots of cases where I reacted too much to pitches I should have laid off of. But if you look at the big picture, yes, I think you can say fouling pitches off made me strike out less.

To make it in the majors, then, it's important to master the technique of staying alive by fouling off pitches you can't turn into hits.

When the situation changes you have to make adjustments.

And having fewer strikeouts is definitely an advantage, isn't it?

That's true. It's a result of reducing the risk factor. But I do admire the players who have a lot of strikeouts. You have to have a lot of confidence to take a big swing at a pitch when you're down 0 and 2.

What about the catchers? Ivan Rodriguez [formerly of the Texas Rangers], reputed to be the best catcher in the majors, kept you from stealing. In Japan had you ever experienced such a powerful arm and quickness in throwing the ball?

No. Never. Never that level of quickness and accuracy. There aren't catchers like him even in the majors.

The first time you played against him he threw you out twice.

I had confidence when I was running, but Ivan's arm beat me. The second time he threw me out was especially a shock.

And the next time you're up against him?

Of course, stealing a base off of him is a goal.

In August in Yankee Stadium they sprayed water on the base path between first and second. Rumor has it that was done as a countermeasure specifically aimed at slowing you down. How did it actually feel to you?

Even if that's true it didn't make any difference. I think you're referring to the fourth inning of the second game of that series when I was thrown out at second base and I didn't slide. Well, let me explain. First of all, that was a hit-and-run, and in that particular case it was almost 100 percent certain that any runner would be out. Just before I got to the base, the fielder already had the ball in his glove, so if I'd tried to slide I clearly would have been tagged out. So I looked for an opening. If you stop in front of second base and look for an opening, an opportunity [an error by your opponent] might present itself. That's why I came to a stop short of the bag. It wasn't that I couldn't slide, but that I chose not to slide.

Do you have a clear understanding with the manager and coaches about what to do in situations where, as a runner, you should hold up or tag up and go?

No, I don't.

So you made those decisions on your own?

Right. You have to do one or the other.

You said you thought you'd be able to excite the fans with your defense. And you did exactly that. The fans were riveted by the way you robbed people of home runs, and by your throws from right field.

I didn't expect them to be that excited. I was surprised myself by their reaction to my defense.

In the eighth inning of your April 11 game against the Athletics, there was one out with a runner on first. The ball dropped into right, and normally you'd expect to end up with runners on first and third, but you fired off a bullet to third. The radio announcer shouted, "A laser-beam strike from Ichiro," and the runner was out. After that your opponents didn't try to run on you so much when the ball was hit to right. Your defense and arm became a real deterrent.

It's definitely an advantage to be able to keep your opponents from running. To get people out on throws like that is in itself a valuable thing, and if they run on you that means that your opponents don't respect your arm.

The official baseballs in Japan and the U.S. feel very different, and I was wondering how major-league balls feel in your hand when you throw them.

They're completely different. They're manufactured differently, out of different materials. I'm completely used to Japanese baseballs and it's hard for me to get used to the balls they use in the majors.

When you threw that laser-beam throw it seemed like you had a good grasp of it.

In that case it fit my hand just right and I got a good grip on it.

Do you sometimes feel like you can't hold it well and it's going to slip?

The balls we use in games have been worked pretty well so

that doesn't happen too much. Brand-new balls I can't get a grasp of at all. They're dry and slippery. The kind of leather they use is completely different, and the stitching is much rougher. Balls in Japan are softer and even new balls fit my hand perfectly.

That announcer's "laser beam" remark was great. Piniella's comment was pretty clever, too; he said, "You could have hung laundry on it." Like your throw followed a taut line [from right to third].

I'm impressed they could come up with those kinds of spontaneous comments.

Playing right field you also turned a few home runs into outs. Are major-league stadiums suited to aggressive defensive plays?

You can be as aggressive as you'd like. You have these nicely cushioned walls, and the height is just right in some places. That height really lets you show your stuff.

The fans sit much closer to the action than in Japan. Are you used to that now?

When the ball comes close to the stands the fans lean over trying to catch it themselves. I understand how they're feeling, but I feel like telling them, "Hey, this is supposed to be my moment to shine." But I'm completely used to this now, the fans being so close.

In the game on May 29 you made that wonderful sliding catch of a fly ball to shallow right to end the game, sliding almost to second base. I remember that fist pump you did.

I didn't do that because I was able to pull off that sliding catch. I did it instinctively because that play ended the game. It was the bottom of the ninth, two outs, runners on first and third. [Kazuhiro] Sasaki was pitching and we were leading by one run. If they got a hit then we'd have to go into extra innings, and they might come back and beat us. So what that gesture meant was "Yes! It's over!"

In the Clubhouse

I wanted to ask about things other than the games. Who do you get along best with on the team?

Everybody's very friendly. I enjoy being with my teammates. In our free time we don't really go out and do things together much, but we do spend a lot of time together, and the whole feeling of the team has helped me a great deal.

I understand you were imitating one of the other players' form just before a game.

Oh, that's right. Boone's batting.

They also made a special holder in the dugout for your bat, didn't they, during the season? A bat rack made out of two tongue depressors, with your name on it.

Coach [John] McLaren did that, all of a sudden. Everybody keeps their bats behind the bench. I don't like that, so during a game I always keep a bat with me on the bench. But it keeps falling over. When I come in off the field I always find my bat knocked over. Coach McLaren noticed that and made this bat rack for me.

Who's been helping you the most with language? Good and bad language.

With English that'd have to be Jay Buhner, Mike Cameron, and Ryan Franklin. For Spanish it'd be Edgar [Martinez], Stan Javier, and Carlos Guillen.

I understand you've spoken to Piniella in Spanish.

Not a real conversation, just simple greetings. With Edgar and Freddy Garcia and the others, the ones who speak Spanish, talking to them in Spanish makes us feel closer. There are lots of players in the majors who speak Spanish. In the American League West Division all the opposing catchers are Spanish speakers. You have Ramon Hernandez of the Oakland A's, Bengie Molina of the Anaheim Angels. And Pudge [Ivan Rodriguez] of the Texas Rangers. I try to decide by their names or faces whether they're English or Spanish speakers, but sometimes when I look at a guy and I think he must speak Spanish, it turns out he doesn't. Once I spoke in Spanish to a guy and it turned out we have the same agent, Tony Attanasio. I later heard he told our agent how surprised he was when I spoke to him in Spanish. That was Homer Bush, second baseman for the Toronto Blue Jays.

How are you doing with languages?

Terrible.

Yumiko: That's not true. He goes out of his way to speak English and Spanish, and that's why he's made so much progress.

What I don't like is when I'm with my teammates facing the

cameras and microphones. I want to go ahead and speak, even if I make mistakes. But once the mike's on me I find I can't say anything.

I read in a Seattle newspaper that you made onigiri [rice balls] for Bret Boone, Yumiko. Is that true?

Yumiko: Yes, I did.

Why was he eating onigiri, of all things? Did he see Ichiro eating them?

In spring training I brought onigiri with me every day and Boone asked me what I was eating. He said, "Could you make some for me tomorrow?" The next day, after he had an onigiri, he hit a home run. After that it was like his lucky charm. "You gotta bring some for me every day," he told me.

How many did you make?

Yumiko: Two. I wrote a "B" on Boone's package so they could tell them apart.

And you'd take them to the stadium, Ichiro?

Yes, in a bag.

What was inside the onigiri?

Pickled plum.

Yumiko: Once he asked me to put something different inside so I put in okaka [thin flakes of dried bonito].

He liked that.

Yumiko: But then he said he wanted pickled plum, so the whole season that's what I made. When I went with my husband when they were playing in San Diego, that was the first time I met Boone, and he thanked me for the onigiri. His wife thanks me every time she sees me. So I keep on making them.

Do you have any hobbies outside of baseball?

This isn't really outside of baseball, but I collect autographed major-league baseballs.

Yumiko: Almost every day he comes back, all smiles, with some new autographed ball. Displaying these balls is my job, but we have so many we're almost running out of space. I wonder what we're going to do with all of them if we get any more, but he keeps on bringing them home. But he looks so happy when he does. Like he's a kid again; he shows me the ball and tells me all about it.

As you live here do you think much about Japan?

The more I live here the more I think that Japan's an amazing place. Everything's so intricate and precise, so convenient there. I think that because America's so spacious, things are more inexact. Even Americans who visit Japan are surprised at how detailed everything is in Japan.

You've said that you wanted to enjoy playing in the majors to your heart's content. It's safe to say you accomplished that, giving it your all. Do you have any thoughts on the future?

As a player I never hold back and am able to thoroughly enjoy playing baseball, but I also think I've learned how to share that enjoyment with those watching the game. Baseball's traditions are kept up by people watching the game at the ballparks. When I see parents and their children, grandfathers and their grandkids coming together to the ballpark, I feel really close to the fans. The same must hold true for those watching the games by satellite relay in Japan.

How about you, Yumiko, the one who's struggled to always be there for Ichiro? You'll be living here in the States for some time from now on.

Yumiko: There was a tough period of adjustment, when I wasn't used to things here. What made me happiest was seeing him going all out to follow his dream. That's why I'm thankful to him. Taking on the challenge of playing in the majors has put a lot of expectations and pressure on him, and my only hope is that he can continue to be happy doing what he wants most to do. And Ichiro's allowed me to share this. I am very grateful for Ichiro letting me be a part of this. His taking up this challenge has made me very, very happy.

You must be very happy yourself, Ichiro, to have such a wonderful partner.

No argument there.

CHAPTER TWO

HITTING THE INSIDE PITCH

Major-League Strike Zone

What are you most conscious of as you've made the transition from Japanese baseball to the major leagues?

First of all, the difference in the strike zone.

It's that different?

There are major differences. The Japanese strike zone tends to favor the inside, while in the American strike zone it's much wider toward the outside. The major-league strike zone is one ball or one and a half balls wider on the outside than in Japan. Actually, since late 1996 during practice I've been consciously thinking about the U.S. strike zone. During batting practice I'd always ask our catcher at Orix Blue Wave, the team I belonged to in Japan, whether a pitch would have been a strike in the majors. This catcher loves the major leagues, is always watching videos of U.S. games, and knows the strike zone over here really well.

Have you ever tried it out in actual games? Deliberately hitting an outside pitch that Japanese would normally call a ball?

I finally felt relaxed enough to do that in the 1999 and 2000 seasons. My batting average was holding steady and psychologically I felt pretty confident, so I did go after some balls outside the strike zone in games. Though not very often.

These were outside pitches that were definitely balls?

That's right.

How did it feel hitting pitches that were balls? And what sort of results did you get?

Mostly I fouled them off. The reason being that I couldn't

ignore all those inside pitches. It wasn't easy at all—concentrating mainly on inside pitches while still going after the outside pitches that would be strikes in the majors.

So you're batting in a strike zone wider than anyone else's.

Since I'd made my own personal strike zone much bigger, I became much more tolerant of the Japanese umpires' calls.

When Japanese umpires called a ball a strike, then, you didn't get upset?

No, I didn't. If they called an outside pitch that was a ball a strike, I just figured OK, I've got to extend my strike zone out to there.

So these close calls became a part of your practice. And that's how you trained your eye and body to get used to the major-league strike zone?

Yes, by the end of the 2000 season, my last in Japan, I'd become very aware of the difference in the two strike zones.

Since joining the Mariners you've been able to actually check out the strike zone over here. What sort of difference, in terms of width, are we talking about?

Every time I step into the batter's box during this spring training I have the catcher call the pitch for me, and even the pitches that are completely outside home plate are all strikes [in the States]. I can't say exactly how many ball widths outside it is, but anything out to the white line of the batter's box for right-handed batters, the line closest to home plate, can be called a strike. This might vary according to the pitcher and the umpire, though.

How did the batting feel to you?

I was able to go after the outside pitches all right. No matter how much your brain tells you a pitch is a strike, if your body's been conditioned to think of it as a ball it's hard to go after it. Even if you manage to make contact, you generally just foul it off. But I'm working on it and hope to overcome that.

America's Asymmetrical Ballparks

How does it feel to play defense at Safeco Field?

I think Safeco and many other American stadiums are pretty asymmetrical, which means you have to keep more on your toes than in Japan. Playing right field here I felt there are going to be a lot more interesting scenarios as an outfielder. The spaces between right center and left center are much deeper than in Japan, which means there's much more ground to cover and more opportunities to show what you can do in the outfield. The walls in the outfield are cushioned and softer, too, which makes for more aggressive play on defense.

At Safeco Field, both in the infield and outfield, you can feel like the fans are right up next to you; the players and the fans are both at eye level with each other. In Japan, protective netting typically surrounds most of the field.

Since there really isn't any netting around the field, the ball flies into the stands the same way it does on the field. The distance between players and the fans is really close, and I've got to get used to that pretty quickly.

Especially the first baseman and third baseman, and the right and left fielders, are so close it's like the fans could almost reach out and touch them. You'll be playing in lots of different stadiums, and it has to be a lot different from playing in Japan.

Yes, the shape of the outfields isn't uniform like in Japan, so there'll be a lot of tricky plays with the ball caroming off the wall. Most of the stadiums here are natural grass, too, which means the roll on the ball will be different in each ballpark. I have to figure this out in each of the stadiums we play in.

The condition of the grass is different in each stadium, isn't it?

There's a million different ways to mow the grass. At Safeco Field the groundskeeper cuts it according to the way the players like it.

So they listen to the players' requests? That means the grass is different for each position.

That's right. It's completely different.

What sort of grass do you like?

As soon as the ball is hit I try to pick up where the ball's going and how it's going to bounce, and I like the grass flat so the speed doesn't change; it's easier to play defense that way.

In Japan it's the exact opposite, with most ballparks for professional games using artificial grass.

That's right.

Do you really play so differently on artificial grass and natural grass?

The stress it puts on your body is very different. You can feel it in your muscles after you make a play. And of course the way you play changes according to the kind of surface. On natural grass you can run as fast as you like, but if you do that on an artificial surface you'll get caught up and there's a good chance you'll get injured, so you tend not to go flat out. The difference in the grass can make baseball more interesting, or less interesting.

If you want to see more exciting baseball, then natural grass is the only choice?

I think so.

During the season you're on the road a lot. Different cities and different fans have an effect on the flow of the game.

The atmosphere can completely change depending on the city you're in. The types of fans, too, can be completely different. I think most of them come to enjoy the game itself, which means the fans are extremely knowledgeable about baseball fundamentals and strategy. Playing before such discerning fans might be a little intimidating, but I'm also looking forward to playing in front of that level of scrutiny.

The way they cheer on the teams, too, isn't all like in Japan.

The impression I get is that all eyes are on the ball.

And they have a seventh-inning stretch when they all stand up and sing "Take Me Out to the Ball Game."

They really love baseball. When you're out there, too, playing, you really get the feeling that baseball is the national pastime.

Reading Pitchers

Talking about your play again, during the season you face some one hundred pitchers. Do you study up on whom you'll be facing?

While I was in Japan I watched broadcasts of major-league games, and now the videos in the Mariners' collection. I've managed to get an idea of the way they throw, the variety of pitches, the trajectories, what kind of off-speed pitches they throw, information that's a lot better than going in completely cold. Just knowing the various pitchers' forms is a help.

This helps you with your timing when you hit the ball?

That's right. Once you know a pitcher's form you can get a mental image of it. To help me with this I've had them make a video showing all the teams in the order we'll be playing them and I've been studying that carefully. But there's a whole lot you can't know until you step into the batter's box and face a pitcher, so what's most important is the information I pick up during the season, while I'm actually batting.

There are all sorts of pitchers who use different strategies, different strikeout pitches, so I imagine it's quite a task to remember all this.

Of course it's a tremendous amount of information, but when it comes to their pitches I've gotten the impression that's a fairly simple matter. It's not all that subtle. The way the pitcher and the battery approach a batter is actually pretty easy to grasp.

Could you be more specific?

Well, when it comes to control, there seem to be more pitchers who are aggressive types than those who are finesse pitchers. I get the feeling there aren't many pitchers who are into brushing the corners of the plate, one ball width inside the plate, one ball width outside. This isn't to say that there aren't pitchers who have impeccable control over balls and strikes, but I think the majority of pitchers here are the type who take more pride in throwing their best stuff rather than trying to manipulate with their delicate control. With that kind of pitcher, if you think too much, trying to predict the kind of pitch that's coming, then you'll definitely miss some hittable pitches. So the most important thing for me is to first decide what kind of pitcher I'm facing—a power pitcher or a finesse pitcher.

When you were playing in Japan you once said, "I don't try to guess what pitches the battery is planning next. I just concentrate on each pitch as it comes, and if I can pick it up carefully with my eyes, then I can hit it." When you play in the majors, then, you haven't changed this basic approach?

That's right. That hasn't changed.

Pitchers in the majors have really individual pitching styles, and seem to pitch their own way. Even if you can pick up the ball it seems like that might throw you off.

There are lots of pitchers who don't even look at the catcher's face when they pitch. They completely look off to the side. Makes you wonder what they're looking at when they pitch. That's a little scary and hard to bat against.

Are there any pitchers like that in Japan?

Hideki Okajima of the Tokyo Giants is the only one I can think of. Looking at the catcher when you pitch is considered such a basic point that if you look to the side in Japan they'll definitely make you change your pitching style.

In the majors do pitchers look off to the side to throw the batter off stride?

I think it's more just out of habit. Part of their rhythm. They think if they look off to the side they'll throw a strike. If they face straight ahead and pitch maybe they'll throw a wild pitch.

One thing that's sure to be surprising in the majors is facing pitchers who throw fastballs clocked at 100 miles per hour.

I'd agree. But if the pitch doesn't have any movement on it, even if it's fast I think I can pick it up. What's more surprising are the breaking balls. The way the curveballs or sliders move or break is unbelievable.

I heard there's one pitch called a biting curve that breaks at an intense angle.

Along with the extreme way they break, they break in different ways depending on the pitcher. It's not a uniform breaking ball. Of course you have your curve, knuckleball, screwball, but also pitches that move like a sinker, too. You also have two-seamer and four-seamer pitches that use the seams of the ball so there's movement on the fastball.

Have you studied what kind of breaking pitches the opposing pitchers tend to use as their strikeout pitch?

I have a basic picture of it.

One time when you were facing Daisuke Matsuzaka of the Seibu Lions, who has the fastest ball in Japan, you said that the moment when you struck out you knew that the next time up you were sure to get a hit. And the next time up you hit a home run. In other words, you don't just think about picking up a pitcher's pitches while you're in the batter's box, but throughout the course of the game.

Of course I concentrate on each pitch as it comes, but I think it's important, even if I strike out swinging, or on a called third strike, not to let it change my mood. If you think, "Oh, I can't hit, I can't cut it," then you won't be able to do anything the next time at bat. Say you don't get a hit three, four times at bat; unless you connect up what you learned with the next time at bat, you'll get out that time, too. Whether you strike out or hit into an out you have to learn something to help you hit next time against that particular pitcher. I always make up my mind, each at bat, not to get all emotional no matter how I do.

There was word that one of your new teammates in Seattle, Kazuhiro Sasaki, cautioned you to be careful about the way you get set in the batter's box. Apparently he said the way you grip the bat with your right hand and wind your arm around in that big sweeping motion, pausing with the bat in front of you pointed forward in the direction of the pitcher, is dangerous because it could be misconstrued as showing up the pitcher, and that you'd better cut it out. Is that true?

Yes, he did warn me to be careful because my approach could be misinterpreted that way.

So are you going to alter the way you get set in the batter's box?

I talked with our batting coach, Gerald Perry, and showed him the way I get set in the box. He said, "In my day, yeah, you'd have been in deep trouble, for sure." But now there probably aren't many pitchers who'd claim that's provoking and get upset about it. He said my style and the way I wind my arm and hold the bat should be OK. Though it apparently isn't a good idea to point the bat at the pitcher and hold it there. Winding my arm around once and then bringing the bat down right away is no big deal. It'd be completely pointless to get a pitcher so mad because I wound my arm around and pointed the bat in his direction that he'd hit me with a pitch, so you can be sure I'll be cognizant not to do it.

Fouling Off Pitches

Have you changed anything about your batting form since you joined the majors?

No, I haven't really made any particular changes.

It seems like you don't lift your leg as much as in Japan, you keep a lower center of gravity, and seem altogether more balanced.

I've been adjusting more where I set up and how I hit depending on the pitcher. When I can't hit in a certain set position, I'll try setting up a little farther back or take a lower stance. Those kinds of things.

Since you're always aware of the major-league strike zone being wider on the outside of the plate, do you wait specifically to hit outside pitches more?

I've never been as conscious of the outside corner of the plate as I am now, and I know I have to go for them, but since those pitches are one or two ball widths off the base, I'm not thinking so much about getting a hit as just getting a piece of it.

Meaning you want to foul them off.

Right. It's really difficult to hit a pitch that's two ball widths off the outside of the plate into fair ground. Because if you don't twist your wrist and rotate your bat, you just can't hit it. So I just try to let the bat make contact and foul the ball off. The kind of pitch I'm really looking for is more an inside pitch. In the beginning of the season I'm sure pitchers will try to test me inside. Home run hitters can even pull outside pitches, but what makes a guy who hits first or second in the order a good batter, someone who's somehow trying to get on base, is the ability to hit inside pitches. So you've got to expect pitchers to see how you can handle that.

I'm sure they'll put you to the test, too.

I'm sure they will—with fastballs. That's the first gauntlet I have to run through. Their pitches are so incredibly fast that if you get labeled as someone who can't hit fastballs inside they'll come at you forever with those.

You can't let it be your weak point.

That's right. And once they start testing me with inside pitches, I want to be able to establish that I can hit them as early into the season as possible.

Is there a technique to avoid dangerous inside pitches?

Yes, there is. The ironclad rule is that if you're going to be hit, let it hit you on the backside of your body. If a super-fast pitch hits you on the front, you can really get injured. You have to avoid that at all costs.

Starting with the 2001 season the entire major league has

started to push for a higher strike zone. I understand the point is to change the way the game seems to give the advantage to hitters over pitchers and also to speed the game up.

That's right. The issue of the length of games is apparently for the fans.

We've talked about the wide strike zone, but how do you feel about the strike zone getting higher?

I think I can handle high pitches. But since it's hard to pick up fast, straight, and high pitches, I have to work on my ability to somehow foul off pitches.

So just like pitches on the outside corner you'll consciously try to foul them off.

When I played for Orix I fouled off pitches when I mishit them, but I rarely fouled off any pitches intentionally.

So learning how to stay alive by fouling off pitches will be one new assignment for you?

I think so. In Japan there are a lot of times when you can get a hit off a ball even if it's on the outside of the plate. But in the majors, a high fastball traveling nearly 100 miles per hour, it's hard to get a hit off of. So here it'll be important to master the art of fouling off pitches.

The way pitchers in the majors pitch from the set position is very different from in Japan, so are there times that makes it hard to hit?

I don't think so. Since they throw from the set position when runners are on base they can't go into a huge windup, which makes it easier for me. There are lots of pitchers who have unique windups, and if they throw from the set position it

From home to first base in 3.6 seconds.

makes it a bit easier for the batter.

So the set position is actually easier for you.

For instance, when Nomo goes into his windup batters are pretty surprised, wondering where in the world the ball's going to be coming from. In the set position, though, there's a lot less movement.

That's how he got the nickname "Tornado," isn't it, from his huge windup? By the way, in the 2000 season with Orix you batted fourth and were expected sometimes to hit home runs. With the Mariners, though, you play a very different role. They want you to get on base, even if it means getting an infield hit or by bunting. Was it hard to switch your way of thinking from being fourth in the lineup to being first or second?

Not really. The specific adjustment is how to respond when the count gets to three balls. Whether you'll swing at the next pitch if it looks like a ball. If you're batting fourth they really want you to hit the ball, so in response to that you'll be aggressive about going after the pitch. You're thinking more of getting a hit or a home run than getting on base by drawing a walk. Now, though, my job is to get on base, so if the count gets to 3 and 0, or 3 and 1, I'll let a pitch that looks like a ball go by. If I'm lucky I'll draw a walk and get on base. I'm sure there'll be a lot more situations like that compared to when I played for Orix.

The Art of the Steal

Once you get on base then you'll start thinking about stealing. With pitchers having such big windups the runner must have a great advantage.

I'm sure I'll try to steal much more than I've done before. The pitcher's form does give you a great advantage. I'll get more chances to steal, and there'll be more situations where I'll have to. When I played for Orix I really kept this to a minimum. With the exception of the '94 and '95 seasons, I generally didn't push myself to try to steal.

With your great speed, why didn't you try to steal more?

With base stealing, how many bases you steal doesn't matter. What matters is in what kind of situation you steal. There are times when stealing a base may help you win the game, and times when it doesn't affect the outcome of the game and only adds to your personal base-stealing stats. Base stealing that helps you get runs, that helps you win, "quality" base stealing, in other words, makes sense, but base stealing that's done just to rack up personal numbers is not my style. There's no meaning in just chasing after your own stats. Especially in the summer in Japan when it's so humid, all it does is wear you out. So I think base stealing means not forcing things, and running when you can definitely get something out of it.

Stealing a base when it's not part of the overall strategy of the game, then, just means trying to improve your own statistics.

If you're going after the base stealing crown, then that's different. But if you just all of a sudden take off on your own, your reputation actually will suffer. People will wonder, "What the heck does that guy think he's doing?"

Have you been in that situation?

After 1996 in Japan, it was less and less necessary for me to steal.

But with the Mariners there are more situations where you feel you have to.

What I do, though, is consult with the coaches to make sure when base stealing is part of the overall team strategy. Of course when they tell me to go for it as much as I want, then that's what I'll do. It's hard, though, when you're told to steal only when there's a 120 percent chance you'll be safe. Since pitchers practice a lot how to prevent steals from the set position. I don't plan to steal when it's like a sink-or-swim-type situation. Even so, no matter how good the catcher's arm, it's impossible to completely prevent a steal. When a catcher makes his usual throw to second and the runner's safe, it always means that the runner has picked up on the pitcher's delivery.

So you don't worry about the catcher's arm so much.

I don't think about the catcher. I worry about the way the pitcher throws.

Even if you don't worry about their arms, what about when they block the plate? That scene we often see when a runner at home on a close play is sent flying by some brawny catcher.

That's the only thing I don't want to do. If you get blocked like that, you'll get worn out. You see it coming—that you'll be sent flying. Botch it and you'll get a serious injury. Also, if you don't time your start perfectly it's really hard to score.

Some catchers pretend to tag you and really smack you one with their mitt, too. With all 250-plus pounds of weight behind them. When you tag up on third, or when you're on second and there's a hit that drops in front of the right fielder, a close play at the plate's unavoidable.

I'm sure there'll be a lot more plays where I tag up. When I'm on second and there's a hit to the outfield, and the third base coach waves his arm and says go for it, get that run. Still, I hope to avoid any collisions at home plate.

Can you picture situations where you'll go for an infield hit to take advantage of your speed?

I can see that happening. 'Cause I think there'll be a lot of changeups thrown to me, what we'd call a forkball in Japan, that sinks on you. Also, with the strike zone wider on the outside of the plate I'll probably hit a lot more infield grounders.

In cases like that I'll try to beat out the throw.

You'll reach base more often, won't you?

I'm not going to go out there, though, trying to raise that percentage by getting infield hits. It's what happens when you try to deal with changeup pitches. I'm not going to change my batting form trying to get infield hits.

But when you do it would mean you got good contact on the changeup.

That's right. Even if it's not a clean hit, you need to be able to make contact.

Defense Strategies

There are thirty teams now in the majors, and the general opinion is that the level of defensive play from outfielders has dropped considerably. I'm sure the designated hitter system has something to do with this, as does the fact that some players are bulking up in an attempt to hit more home runs, and they say that many players are slow on their feet. One American journalist has written that "someone like Ichiro, an outfielder who's great on defense, is the kind of player the major league needs most."

I'm really happy to hear that. Some outfielders who aren't that good defensively, though, are often home run hitters, aren't they? That's one goal for them, and they're responding to what the fans want, so it's hard to generalize about whether it's good or bad. The infielders, though, are something else. The way they move on defense is simply amazing, and most of the time I'm really impressed by them.

The infielders' fielding may be brilliant, but there aren't many outfielders like you.

I think one way I've surprised the fans in America is with my defense and my throwing. That might be the biggest factor.

When they see the range you cover on defense and how great your arm is, I can imagine the fans will get pretty excited.

I always look forward to the way the fans in the right field stands react. I like how excited they get. The last few years in Japan I didn't get that reaction from the crowd, because they've taken a kind of "been there, seen that" attitude toward my defensive play.

Do you gather reports on how the other batters hit, like "This player hits a lot in the medium-distance range," or "This player hits a lot of home runs to right and center"?

That's a concern of mine. Not simply information about their batting average or kind of hits, but more detailed data about how they hit with certain pitchers, or what kind of hits they get with certain types of pitches. When major leaguers hit the ball there's a special kind of spin on it, and a lot of power. There's no end to it once you try to analyze it. I've experienced how tough it is to field them sometimes.

What makes them hard to field?

They each have their own individual style of batting. You can really see the effects of the different styles in the way the ball come off the bat. There are a lot of players who really drive the ball, and a lot of players who hit it in a way that makes it go farther than you expect it to. There's definitely a lot to pay attention to.

Before each game do you talk with the manager and coaches about strategy?

Besides our normal team meeting before a game, if there's something I want to check I always go right away to ask them. About how I should handle tricky plays and so on.

Can you give me an example of what you ask about?

You'll always have a situation in a game where you have to make a choice of how to make a certain play. It's really important for a player to clearly understand how his team wants to approach that situation. For example, say there are no outs, a runner on second, and there's a deep fly to the outfield. You're not sure if it'll be caught, or get through for a hit. If it gets through it's a certain double. If I were the runner, then what should I do? Should I wait near the bag so I can easily tag up, or should I go halfway down the baseline so that if it gets through I can score? If you don't make sure of how they want you to handle that and you're thrown out it'll be your own fault and they'll all wonder what the heck you were doing. In the case where there are no outs and I'm on second and stay close to the bag, if the next batter gets a double I can only advance to third. But if I go halfway down the baseline I'll be able to score. There'll be a definite choice of one or the other, depending on how the team wants to play it. I would let them know I'd like a clear sign of how they want me to play it.

It's the delicate situations where you need to make certain of things the most.

If they give me a clear sign and tell me what to do, then that's fine. But when there's no sign and the player's blamed for the out, it'll affect how much they trust you during a game.

Do the Mariners coaches really listen to you?

They're very serious about listening to me.

Bats and Spikes and Gloves

I want to ask you about the equipment you're using now. The Mariners-colored spikes are really cool. They really stand out.

They do, don't they? They match the uniform really well, and I like them a lot. How we look is important. I want to wear the kind of spikes that young kids who play baseball think, "Wow, I want to have those; I want to wear those." It's vital for baseball to have that kind of appeal.

I hear that you've had new spikes made especially for you to use in the majors.

I have. The main thing about them is how light they are. To me, the ideal situation is to feel like I'm almost running barefoot when I wear them. If they're too heavy it doesn't feel like my own feet somehow. I asked them to make them especially light, and they came up with a new material for the shoes, which are only 150 grams [5.3 ounces] per shoe, if you can believe it. They're the best spikes I've ever worn. Up till now when I wore spikes I felt like I wanted to change them for sneakers, but now it's the other way around. The spikes feel so good that when I have sneakers on I want to change to the spikes.

Did it take a long time for them to develop these spikes?

Yes, it did. But I'm a 100 percent satisfied with them. The people at Asics, a sports equipment maker in Japan, were good enough to listen to all sorts of requests I had. The spikes I wore up till last year were leather soles with metal spikes, but the ground in major-league stadiums is much harder than in Japan, so if you run with those spikes the soles of your feet start to hurt. In order to solve this I had them change from a leather sole to a plastic resin one. Now I have both types of shoes, which use the same new material for the uppers.

So you wear one kind or the other depending on the conditions?

The lightest ones are the ones with leather soles. If I'm moving around a lot, though, the plastic resin ones feel better, so I think I'll wear that kind the most over here.

Did you have your gloves and bats made by the same people who made them for you when you were with Orix?

Yes. My gloves are made by Mr. Nobuyoshi Tsubota of Mizuno, another sports equipment company in Japan. The bats are made by Mr. Isokazu Kubota. He's from Mizuno, too.

Did you make any changes to your equipment before coming to the majors?

I changed the color.

To what color?

My gloves are blue, the bats black.

So it's OK to color your bats in the majors?

Actually black bats have been allowed in Japan for several years, but I never liked the black they used. It's kind of a light black. The regulations don't let you make it jet black the way I like it.

In the majors there are no regulations about color, then.

Since you can make the bats exactly the color you like, I've had them paint them black the way I like them.

Does changing the color have an effect on them?

When they make bats they polish them, and when they make them black they usually are polished only once, but I have them do it twice. It comes out looking really black and strong.

Major leaguers play a lot more games than in Japan, so how many bats do you have ready to use?

I don't think any other [Japanese] player's ordered as many bats as I have. When I'm in America I can't get new ones right away, so I'm thinking of having about 150 made. Normally at a home game, I'll have seven or eight ready to choose from, but when I go on away games I'll have twice that many with me in a case.

Japanese Baseball

Now that you're playing in the majors you probably have a better view of Japanese baseball, I imagine. Are there good points about baseball in Japan?

The main thing is the feeling of gratitude. The way players feel toward their equipment and the baseball field itself. Players here don't help rake the ground or polish their spikes or gloves. In the majors you always have groundskeepers, equipment managers, even people who clean the dirt off your spikes, but I just can't get used to that way of doing things. Of course, we have professional groundskeepers and equipment managers in Japan, too. But we sometimes rake the grounds and polish our gloves by ourselves. That's the way we express our gratitude. That's one of the good points of Japanese baseball, I believe.

What about baseball techniques?

When it comes to physical ability Japanese players are no match for major leaguers, so they have to make up for that with a feel for details. The ability to judge what kind of hit it'll be by watching the bat and ball the moment they strike each other, the ability to predict from the spin of the ball the direction it'll go—nobody can beat the Japanese in the attention they pay to the intricacies of the game. Major leaguers, even if they don't have that kind of sense for details, can get by with their speed and power.

But if major leaguers started paying more attention to the details of the game . . .

If they could do that, it'd be amazing. No one would be able to touch them. There are a lot of players I see and I think if they only paid a little more attention to the intricacies they'd be fantastic.

Since you know the differences between the two approaches to baseball, you should be able to put the best of American elements and Japanese elements together.

I'd like to, as far as my play is concerned. No matter how much I get used to playing in the majors, though, I don't want to forget that feeling of gratitude. I'll continue to clean my own glove and spikes.

Do you use any dietary supplements to stay in shape?

I've been taking those since I played for Orix. Just protein supplements, amino acid, vitamins, and the like.

Along with supplements, do you do any form of mental training? Watching videos of your own plays over and over, or meditation or something?

Nothing in particular, really. If I had to list anything, I guess it would be the fact that I try not to take in any information. What I mean by information is Japanese sports newspapers and magazines. If I start worrying about how the Japanese media are looking at me, it'll give me a lot of stress. It's easy to say you won't let negative opinions get to you, but they never work out to be a plus factor for you. This isn't exactly a type of training, but it is something I'm very conscious of.

So you don't read any sports newspapers or magazines at all?

If I'm not playing, like say I'm laid up with an injury or something, I do read them, but during the season I hate to have them anywhere in sight.

I'm sure people have told you that since you're a star you can't stop them from writing about you.

Of course I understand that. And it's fine for readers to enjoy reading those. I just don't like getting influenced by things that aren't true.

Finally, as one of your fans, I picture you playing in the All-Star Game.

I can't picture that at all, myself. But if it does happen someday, it'll be a big responsibility.

CHAPTER THREE

WHY I CHOSE THE MAJORS

Japan-U.S. Games

I'd like to turn to the question of why you decided to move over to the majors, and get the background to that decision.

Well, there were a few reasons. It was a decision that put my career as a baseball player on the line, that's for sure.

What was it that first sparked your interest in joining the majors? I understand that after you played in the Japan-U.S. baseball games in 1996 you really could feel how great Major League Baseball is.

The excitement I felt in that series was definitely a turning point. Instead of just something I admired from afar, the majors became a set goal of mine.

There were so many fantastic players on the Major League Baseball team you played against then.

Cal Ripken, Jr., Mike Piazza, Alex Rodriguez, Barry Bonds, Brady Anderson, Pedro Martinez, Pat Hentgen—an unimaginable combination of players. I get excited now just thinking about it. Alex Rodriguez said it best: "It's an honor just to play with such superstars."

What impression did you get watching them play?

I remember it really well. I'd watched major-league games on TV, but this was the first time for me to really experience their speed and power. It was the first time for me to really see up close the kind of pitches they throw, the way they bat, to feel how good they really are. The pitchers' form was completely different from in Japan. I remember feeling in awe. Though I wasn't all that surprised by the actual pitches. The speed wasn't particularly overpowering. But the position players were really different from those in Japan. There's their power, of course, but I also felt the way they bat is different. Of course the strike zone is different, but I was under the impression that they go after pitches that are balls more often. But actually when I watched them bat up close, I saw they didn't do that at all. They have a really outstanding batting eye. Also, from the first pitch they're ready to swing. Whether it's a forkball or a curve, they take a healthy swing at it. They don't just let it go by. Even if they miss, they react to the ball and swing at it. They step into it and swing with everything they've got. This is very different from Japanese batters. Even with the kind of big curve that the veteran Nobuyuki Hoshino [now of the Hanshin Tigers] throws, major-league batters took a huge swing at it, and never pulled back from it. They give you this strong sense from the very first pitch that they came to hit the ball. They're going to take the initiative when it comes to swinging the bat, and they're not about to let the pitcher make them swing. I was quite surprised by this. I realized that if you have your body and batting form the way you want them, you can face up to any pitcher.

So you started to see your own play in light of theirs?

When I saw them, my simple reaction was just that Major League Baseball play is really something else, that there are so many great things about it. I thought what a great feeling it was to be able to be with these players who always gave their best, players who feel this way about the game. And it got me excited to think about how even better they must be in regular-season games. That could be said about the pitchers, too.

So you didn't see Major League Baseball as something completely out of reach.

In the off-season when it was time to renew my contract, I told a person in my organization that Major League Baseball was something I was interested in for the future. But he just laughed it off. He wasn't making fun of me, it's just that at that time it probably didn't seem like a thought he needed to occupy his time with.

Did it hurt that he didn't take it seriously?

I just thought OK, that's the way it is. All of a sudden coming out and saying you want to play in the majors, it's no wonder he laughed.

Did the person you talked to happen to be Katsutoshi Miwata, the scout for your team and the one who found you among thousands of high school players, who passed away three years ago?

That's right. I don't know how he really felt about it at the time, but when I mentioned it to him, he just laughed.

But I'm sure Mr. Miwata, the one who discovered you, would have been happier than anyone else that you've now joined the Mariners. By the way, during that same year, 1996, in the Pacific League, which Orix belongs to, the showdowns between you and Hideki Irabu became a real drawing card. His pitching was more effective then than his pitching recently in Major League Baseball. You stated publicly that you looked forward to these showdowns, but in the 1996 off-season, when Irabu moved to the Yankees, didn't this bring about a change in your thoughts about going to the majors?

There really aren't that many exciting moments where it's a one-on-one encounter, pitcher versus batter, rather than one team against another. When Irabu was on the mound, of course I wanted our team to win, but I was also excited trying to hit his pitches. And it was a bit of a letdown once I realized that, with his move to the majors, I wouldn't be able to bat against him again. I'd always tried to keep myself motivated to hit against him, but this took a sudden nosedive. Which doesn't mean, though, that his moving to the majors had any direct effect on my own move.

So moving to the majors was your own personal issue, then.

I think so. I really looked forward to seeing how Irabu did with the Yankees, and I expected that players in the majors would have trouble hitting his fastball that I knew only too well. I felt the same way when Nomo went to the Dodgers a few years earlier than Irabu. When I batted against him in Japan he wasn't at his peak, but I knew all about his forkball and fastball.

After the Japan-U.S. games and the '97 pennant race started, did you feel even more drawn to the majors?

No, I was too involved in taking a good, hard look at my own batting. I just didn't have the leisure to consider it. It was like I was taking one step forward, then one step back. Every single day was a struggle for me because I just wasn't hitting the way

I wanted to. But one thing positive I could get out of this situation was this: even with my far-from-perfect batting I was able to do OK against the major leaguers, so if and when I was able to get to the point where I was satisfied with my batting I should be able to do even better. That thought kept my spirits up.

In the 1996 Japan-U.S. games your batting average was .636. Seven hits in eleven at bats, and two stolen bases. It seems your performance at bat and your feelings about the majors were at odds with each other.

I guess so. Which made me all the more want to get my batting the way I wanted it to be. I wanted to get to the point, as soon as I could, where I could bat the way I wanted to, with confidence.

The Turning Point

For two weeks starting on February 23, 1999, you participated in the Seattle Mariners training camp in Peoria, Arizona. Was this the opportunity that made you want to join the majors?

That was an exciting time for me. I was able to see Ken Griffey, Jr., and Alex Rodriguez again. Physically and mentally I started aiming to join the majors after the opening of the 1999 season.

So something major happened in the 1999 season to bring this on?

That's right. Nineteen ninety-nine was a turning-point year

for me. As an outfielder I became a changed man. There was a quantum leap as far as my batting was concerned, and in my feelings about the majors.

So it was a turning point.

Exactly.

Starting with your batting, what change did you experience?

I got tremendous confidence in my batting. I don't know where my peak is as far as batting goes, but I know I'll never be in a slump again.

Why can you be so confident about that?

Early in the '99 season something just clicked. I could finally get hold of a certain feeling I'd been looking for. Once that clicked in I knew I'd never lose it again. Which is why I can say that. It was a dramatic change for me.

So there was a major transformation in your batting?

There was. Very clearly I took it to another level.

I'd like to hear more about that.

This might be a little long, but the first thing I need to talk about is what people consider the yardstick of my batting, my batting average. I'm certainly proud of being the top batter in Japan seven years in a row, and I really think I did a good job. But the only years I was satisfied with my batting were my first year, 1994, and 1999 and 2000. The four years '95 to '98, it was a constant struggle to get to the top. I don't think many people are aware of this, though. People kept praising me, saying how great my batting was, but believe me, over and over I felt like I was thrown into the pits of despair. I continually had to push myself by telling myself just to do it. In the end I was able to produce good batting averages, but those numbers hid the deep despair I was secretly feeling over my batting. My feelings toward the fans and their support and the responsibility I had for the team encouraged me, but more often than not I was very self-critical and struggled terribly. During the seven years I played for Orix, I often felt lost and, deep down, never really believed in my abilities as a ballplayer.

That's really hard to believe, that the top batter in Japanese baseball would struggle like that.

It wore me out. It was terrible and I often felt like I was going to fall apart. If this was just a question of psychological turmoil or depression I think I could have handled it. But I was struggling with the technical aspects of hitting, and I couldn't find any way to switch gears to be more positive. I did my best despite my confusion, as I fought to squeeze out every last ounce of strength. And the numbers I came up with ended up putting me in the top spot as a batter.

So despite winning the top batting prize year after year you were never satisfied with your batting.

Nineteen ninety-four, my first full year up from the farm team, I thought I did a good job. It was all like a dream, but I gave it 120 percent. But the four years after this I wasn't satisfied with my play at all. I felt like I was playing at only half my real ability.

If that's true, that means you were able to set those batting average records with only half of what you're capable of.

Which made it all the more frustrating. I'm capable of so much more, I was sort of yelling to myself, so why is this all I can do?

You had such a firm hold on the top batting crown, and always looked like you were at the top of your game. I never imagined that you were struggling so very much.

It was a physically painful feeling that you can't put into words. I was just angry all the time.

But during the '99 season you were freed from this painful situation.

That's right. In the beginning of the season I was able to grasp that feeling that's the core of my batting.

If I remember right, you were in a terrible slump at the beginning of the season.

That's right. During spring training I trained as much as I possibly could, but from the first game of the new season something was different. I just couldn't hit. When I went after a pitch, just before I hit it I couldn't follow it with my eyes. Batters don't just hit with their bodies, but you zero in on the ball coming toward you with your eyes, and the information you pick up visually is what you use to make contact with your bat. In other words, before you hit [with your body] you're already hitting [with your eyes]. And that's what I couldn't do at the time.

That's a fatal flaw, wouldn't you say, if a batter can't pick up the pitch?

You can hit only when the information picked up by your

optic nerve is processed by your brain and then transmitted accurately to your body. If your eyes can't pick it up, then you can forget about good results.

So the instant that the ball passes in front of you, you pick it up with your eyes. Do the kinds of pitches and speed of the pitch have an impact when you can't pick up the pitches well? I imagine if it's a super fastball or tremendous breaking pitch you might not be able to pick them up.

No, when I'm batting well that doesn't make much of a difference. As long as it's in the strike zone I can pick up almost any ball.

So why couldn't you?

It's a matter of my whole swing and timing. I might have been feeling a little pressure with the season just starting. Since I couldn't follow the ball even when it's right over the plate there was no way I was going to get a hit. I heard people around me say, "Something's the matter with Ichiro this year." I hated to hear those kind of remarks. I tried to hone my senses because they were rusty. But I never thought of giving up, I can tell you that. It was a terrible slump but I was confident I'd be able to get my batting back.

And then the moment came when you could grasp that special feeling.

It was April 11, 1999, a Sunday at the Nagoya Dome, a game against the Seibu Lions. The last game of a three-game series. It was the ninth inning, I was the leadoff batter, Yukihiro Nishizaki was the relief pitcher, and I hit this clumsy grounder to second. Especially for a left-handed batter, grounding out to the second baseman's right side is awful. It's better to hit it to the center-field side of the second baseman. My hit was the worst kind of grounder to second, but the instant after I hit it, it was like a mist cleared up before my eyes. "That's it!" I thought. "This is what I've been looking for!" The timing and swing I'd been searching for I found in that instant. This wasn't some vague image, but something I could grasp totally with my mind and body.

So that was a pretty dramatic moment for you. But how could such a terrible grounder to second lead to the answer you'd been looking for?

I'm not really sure. . . . Probably it was the result of so many continuing failures. Like they say, every failure is a stepping stone to success. In that game up until the ninth inning I hit into easy outs three times out of the four times I was at bat, but I wasn't looking into the causes of my poor batting. But this final at bat when I hit the grounder to second, this very strange sensation came over me. My own theory is that in this fifth time at bat I was completely able to pick up the pitch. So the chances were extremely high it'd be a hit. In reality, though, it ended up a simple grounder to second.

So there was a gap between the image you had and reality.

That's right. It was clear to me that something was wrong. I tried to find the answer right away. During the few seconds it took me to run to first, I put the mental image I had of my batting form and the actual form that grounded out to second together in my mind, like trying to solve an equation. And it all came to me, clear as a bell. It was the first time as a ballplayer that such a clear answer had come to me. I felt like jumping up and down, I was so happy.

I imagine nobody understood how you could be so happy at grounding out to second.

That's right. The manager was pretty upset when I got back to the dugout. With that final grounder to second my average had slipped to .223. But I was so filled with that sensation of having captured that special feeling that I couldn't help smiling. That smile only made my manager even more upset. The next day was a travel day so we were supposed to be off from practice, but once we got to the town where we were playing next I was dragged off to do some batting practice. If I'd been hitting .350 then I could have had a day off.

I'd like to get to the crux of the matter, namely that certain feeling you said you were able to grasp. What was that, exactly?

It's extremely hard to talk about it, since it's a personal feeling. Basically since the way I bat is unusual, I can't explain it to other people.

But if you absolutely had to put it into words . . .

Well, how could I put it? . . . It's really hard to explain. It's a way of adjusting what's off in the way you use your body when you're in the midst of an at bat, and in the instant when you hit the ball. There's a focal point for both the upper half of the body and the lower half. In order to correct what's off, the way you use the lower half of your body is critical. To be a bit more specific, it has to do with the way I use my right foot and the angle at which I step into the pitch. If that angle is off, then even if you think you're able to get to the ball perfectly, you'll end up hitting into an easy out.

The actual difference in distance you're talking about is just a matter of a few centimeters?

Maybe less than that, even. Several millimeters, perhaps. And maybe not even that much. The batting form might look exactly the same, but there's a subtle margin of error involved.

What do you mean by a subtle margin of error?

This is also hard to explain. In simple terms, something goes out of whack with the movement you make that allows you to hold back and follow the ball for a longer period of time, and the movement you make that allows you to concentrate your energy at the point of impact.

But even if other players were to watch they wouldn't pick up on whatever's wrong, would they?

That's exactly right. The style of batting that I demand of myself is impossible to completely implement if there is even so much as a tiny error that's so subtle it's undetectable to the naked eye. Therefore, I need some kind of sensor to help me identify what's off in my batting. Thanks to that seemingly meaningless ground out to the second baseman, the internal sensor I needed was somehow magically activated. With that, I was able to come into possession of the special feeling that now allows me to correct any flaws in my batting. I don't believe there could ever be any greater stroke of luck. It's possible

I could have gone through my entire career fruitlessly searching for that feeling without ever having found it.

So that very keen sense allows you to get to the bottom of any flaws, and that's what lies behind your batting.

Baseball is a much more delicate sport than you'd ever imagine. And let me tell you, this concept doesn't just apply to me. Other players, too, have their own particular state of mind, each of them very demanding of themselves when they come to play, and with their own special feeling that's indescribable to other people.

Looking at your statistics, I see that after April 11, 1999, your batting average went way up. Your batting does seem to have changed since that grounder to second.

It did, most definitely. There was a period of trial and error, but never again did I feel like there was no light at the end of the tunnel. Up till then I'd felt like I drifted in and out of grasping that feeling, but now it's as tangible as a mathematical theorem, something I can grasp very clearly. Since I now have the confidence that I'll never be lost again, I won't ever be as anxious as I was in the past. I've taken my batting to another level. During the 1999 and 2000 seasons I could grasp that more and more with each time at bat.

So it was more fun for you to bat.

I've enjoyed it ever since. To a certain extent baseball's the kind of sport where the stats control you. Through 1998, even though I led the league in batting every year, I always felt pressured by [batting average] stats. But this changed starting in

'99. I was able to reduce all the stats to just another element in the overall picture and get on with playing the game.

An unbelievable evolution you went through.

In the '98 season whenever I stepped into the batter's box I felt I could make contact with 50 percent of the strikes thrown. But after that grounder to second in April '99, that percentage went up by 10 percent to 20 percent; in other words, I felt I was able to hit 70 percent of the strikes thrown.

That's an amazing figure.

Obviously I'm biased, and even though I think it's fun to watch the pitcher, as a sport, batting's really the main attraction. Batting takes a high level of technique developed over time, and requires a demanding level of physical ability and skill that's as much as you'd find in any other sport. If you're off just a little bit, it's hard to have even a 30 percent success rate. Almost impossible, in other words, to be successful three times out of ten. Even if you're close to perfect, you won't bat .400. No matter what fantastic technique a batter might have, 60 percent of the time he'll fail. This shared understanding can actually work to the batter's advantage. But if you lean on that advantage and step into the batter's box thinking you'll fail more often that you'll succeed, there's no way you'll get anywhere near .400. Which is exactly why, in the 2000 season, I was tremendously aware of the figure .400.

It's unprecedented for anyone to bat .400 in Japan, but you set out to do it anyway.

I set out to get as close to .400 as I could. Finally, I felt everything

I needed to do to achieve that level was in place. I felt that if I was able to make contact with 60 to 70 percent of the strikes thrown to me, hitting .400 wasn't out of the realm of possibility.

During your final season with Orix you hovered between .350 and .400. For a batter that gap between the two must seem huge.

It does seem that way. In the '99 season, while I felt confident that my batting was finally evolving, I had to content myself with a .343 average. I felt I could squarely hit more than 70 percent of the strikes but, in the end, I fell short of .350. I had too many mishits. I knew that if only I could cut down on the number of mishits, I could boost my average much higher.

Those mishits definitely did go down, and in the 2000 season for a time you were batting .400, and even with your injury you ended up with a much higher batting average than the previous season, .387. I've got to ask, though, what you mean by mishits.

It simply means when you're sure up until the moment of contact, that the swing you've made is good enough for a hit, but it doesn't turn out that way. Instead, you foul the ball off or pop it up or something like that because of a momentary breakdown in your form or because you're straining too much. The vast majority of these are careless misses. Not that they can't be hit, but that you obviously mishit them. That's why it's so incredibly frustrating and it makes me so upset.

In '99, then, you vastly improved your ability to get to pitches. But pitchers have a lot of ways to throw a batter off stride. Combining fastballs and changeups, trying their best to mix up pitches to outwit the batter. It becomes a kind of psychological battle, and when you say you can get to a pitch, does this mean you've figured out what the battery is planning in terms of pitches?

If you could do that, then you could really hit with a lot more certainty. Gambling everything on being able to read what kind of pitch is coming, though, means there's a high chance you'll be wrong, so it's risky. It's too dangerous to rely too much on guessing what kind of pitch it'll be or reading what kind of course it'll follow. I'm only about 30 percent conscious of the type of pitch. The other 70 percent I'm concentrating on picking up the ball as an object—no matter what kind of pitch it is or course it takes.

So you need to maintain a seven-to-three balance.

That's right. For example, if the ball doesn't follow the course you've gambled on and you think you'll mishit it, if you focus on picking up the ball you'll be able to stay alive by getting a piece of it and fouling it off. Then you can wait for the next chance.

You can create your own opportunities.

That's what makes a strong batter, I think, one who can work the count.

Have your reflexes ever gotten in the way—you're waiting for your pitch but your body reacts anyway and you hit the ball?

Yes, that happens. There've been a lot of times when I'm not planning on hitting a pitch but I end up hitting it anyway. My head knows not to swing, but my body thinks it can get a hit and swings away. When that happens as I'm running the bases I'm thinking, "Darn! I shouldn't have hit it!" It's my body, not my brain, that's doing the batting at times like these, but surprisingly, a high percentage of those turn into hits.

I remember the game against the Chiba Lotte Marines on May 13, 2000, when Toshiyuki Goto threw a pitch that bounced just in front of the plate and surprisingly you turned it into a hit.

That was a hit where the body just reacts. The opposite happens, too. Where your brain tells you to hit but your body just won't go for it.

Why is that?

It's a strange thing, but when a pitch is too perfect to hit you can get scared, and strain too much. It's not the pitcher who goes right down the middle with a pitch, which is a risky strategy to throw the batter off. It's almost always the catcher who calls that. For a batter it's never a one-on-one fight, but always one against two.

So it's reading too much into it, then, to say that if a batter lets a pitch right down the middle go by he's merely letting a fat pitch go by.

Instead of saying the batter let the pitch go by, you should say he was made to let it go by. Hats off to the opposition there. No need to pretend you did it purposely; they got you. In my case, when a pitch comes right down the middle I feel like "How about I smack that one for a home run?" When I feel like that, though, I end up not hitting it cleanly, but strain too much and slice the bat under the ball and pop up to the catcher. What should go over the fence ends up going straight up in the air. In the 2000 season for Orix, when I was batting fourth, there was always a very fine line between hitting a home run and popping up to the catcher.

Now that you're a member of the Seattle Mariners can we expect your batting to evolve even more?

Ever since the 1999 season I've had the strong sense that now I can hit, now I can bat the way I want to. In 2000 I felt that the basic foundation I need as a batter was now in place. I don't think that foundation will crumble at all. My job now is to see how I can apply all that in a new environment, the majors. Of course, that's an assignment that has no end.

You were struggling to discover the kind of batting you wanted for so long, then in 1999 you were able to find it and you could start to really enjoy batting. Compared to when you first started thinking of going over to the majors, in 1996, your feelings and play are completely different, aren't they, in 2001, now that you've actually been able to move over to the majors?

That's really true. After '99 my motivation for moving to the majors completely changed. Before that, whenever I thought I wanted to play in the majors it was because I wanted to find a change of environment and escape from the troubles I was having, where nothing seemed to be working out. I thought that something good would come out of a change of venue. But now I don't have those negative feelings at all. Quite simply I want to take the self-discoveries I've made in my batting and put it all to use at the highest level of baseball in the world. My goal is that simple.

Crisis for Japanese Baseball

When I talked with you in 2000 you said, "No matter how much I might try I might not be able to please the fans more than I am now." I couldn't get those words out of my mind. Even when you were going for your seventh straight batting title and trying to bat .400, the sad fact was that your home stadium, Kobe Green Stadium, wasn't filled. For a player like you, who while always trying to win is also motivated by trying to give the fans your very best, how do you feel about the fact that over the past few years baseball's been drawing fewer and fewer fans in Japan?

Naturally I wanted those who come to the stadium to watch baseball to enjoy my improvement. But I couldn't figure out how to draw those fans who weren't coming anymore back to the stadium. Of course for fans who want their team to win, winning's the best way, but for those who come to the game looking for me to do something, if they come to the stadium but don't feel they're getting what they came for, there's not much I can about it. Because I was giving it all I had.

Maybe the Orix fans got too used to you winning all those batting titles and challenging the sacred .400. Could they have lost sight of your appeal?

Whatever the reason, the number of fans was declining. If I'd been hitting .450 or .500, with fifty home runs, maybe a few more fans would have come. While batting fourth, if I'd started as pitcher and won ten games, maybe we could have drawn more people. A lot of unlikely scenarios like that went through my mind. But that would just be a temporary fix. A kind of a fad. People get caught up in trends like that, but they give them up just as quickly. That's what hurts the most.

Even when you stepped into the batter's box batting .400 the stadium wasn't full.

The number of fans gradually decreased.

Have you ever thought that interest in you was just a passing fad, too?

I have. In '94, when I got my 200th hit that season [the first 200-hit season in the history of Japanese baseball], there were lots of fans who came to see me play. We were playing a game against the Nippon Ham Fighters at the end of the season in the Tokyo Dome that was essentially meaningless because both teams were out of the pennant race, but we filled the place with 50,000 fans. Something you'd never normally see happen. I had a very strong sense that I wanted to live up to the fans' expectations. Partly due to this, the next year I started to feel a lot of pressure and stress. The Kobe earthquake in January 1995, though, made us even more determined to win the pennant for the embattled area, and Orix really got on a roll. I felt very strongly that once we'd gotten to the top we couldn't let ourselves fall back. After winning the Japan Series in '96, though, attendance started to dwindle. Which really made me feel that it's quite limited what one individual can do.

Did your other teammates feel the same way?

I really don't know.

But you felt a lot of individual responsibility?

Well, it's true that the past few years I've been wracking my brain trying to think of what I might do to improve the situation.

Did you think that your play wasn't a drawing card to bring in the fans?

I did. Most of the time, though, I felt they were looking for me to do something. I could understand how they'd want to come to the stadium if only I could get to 210 hits, tying the season-high record in Japan I set in '94, just to see number 211.

There should have been throngs of fans coming to the stadium who wanted to see how you were doing.

The drop-off in the number of fans coming to see the games, though, means that more and more people are looking to the players for something other than baseball.

A lot more fans see baseball players as heroes or idols, don't they?

That's right. There are a lot of people who come to the stadium like they're chasing after a movie star or something. But one thing's true, though. That's helped save Japanese baseball today. The stadiums fill up with people who want to see the players they've seen on TV. If those kind of fans stopped coming to the stadium, we'd have even lower attendance.

Is the quality of baseball falling off?

It's a harsh thing to say, but it's true. The past few years people have been saying that Japanese baseball's in a crisis. But that's not a recent phenomenon. Baseball as a sport has been in a rut for a long time. The players and teams must be aware of this, but still they reassure themselves saying things like

"Well, at least we're still more popular than professional soccer."

The Tokyo Giants, of course, are the team with the greatest influence in all of Japanese baseball. They have the most financial power, the biggest draw among the fans, and the greatest coverage in the media. Japanese baseball in a real sense revolves around the Giants. They're the symbol of baseball in Japan, and I wondered what you think about them.

The Giants are what keep Japanese baseball going, no doubt about it. Both in terms of popularity and financially. Someone like me who was playing for Orix has reaped the benefits of this, and I'm quite aware of the high position they hold. Though I don't think that the idea that you'll have influence and be able to do anything as long as you have money is a good lesson to teach children.

Getting the best players is where money talks.

Yes, but as far as baseball goes, recruiting the best players or whatever as a way of winning is accepted, so that's not really an issue. I think we need a team like the Giants. With a team like that with such overwhelming popularity, of course this will spawn an anti-Giants movement, and because the Giants are there it raises the tension level in the games. If all the baseball teams just turned into colorless local teams, that would be boring.

Japanese baseball undoubtedly needs the Giants more than any other team. But isn't the level of popularity they draw leading to a decline in the quality of baseball?

It definitely is a double-edged sword. The fans are extremely important. I certainly understand that. This may be a little bit of an exaggeration, but the stance of baseball right now is that if you can get 40,000 fans in the stadium then it's succeeded as entertainment. I have no problem with people picking a player as their idol and getting all excited about him. But if that continues for long players get used to it in a bad sense of the term. That popularity should bring a sense of tension and expectancy in the players, but that's been endlessly watered down. Fans who like baseball come to the stadium to see plays that only professional ballplayers can execute. And the players' pride as professionals spurs them on to want to display some brilliant plays for those who come to see them. As long as the players diligently apply themselves behind the scenes, then baseball should be fun to watch. The question is whether or not players are conscious of this.

If what you say is true, it's a serious problem. It would mean that baseball isn't enjoyable for the fans to watch.

It really is a serious problem in Japan. It's a question of players' attitudes. In addition to your bottom-line goal of winning, I think professional ballplayers also have a duty to let people who buy tickets enjoy a high level of play. There isn't as strong an awareness of this, though, as there should be.

In the past Japanese baseball could be really exciting.

That's true. But something's different now. You have to figure out what kind of play will attract fans, what will keep their interest alive. Japanese baseball has been driven into a dangerous position. I always gave it everything I had, but if you asked me whether I enjoyed playing ball, I'd have to say no. I didn't know what to do with myself when I found it boring.

Respect

Almost all the ballplayers who are on the twelve Japanese professional baseball teams were among the elite players in high school or college. In America, the majors stand at the pinnacle, but there's a broad lower base below that, and you have to claw your way up from the Rookie League to A, AA, and Triple A if you want to play in the majors. Only the rare player jumps directly from high school or college to the majors. For the rest, it's like a fight where only the strongest survive and move up to the next level. But in Japan, for instance, if a player felt embarrassed about scraping it out under those circumstances, then he probably could survive without playing that way.

Unfortunately, you're right about that. Since I've come to America I've begun to think there really is a huge difference between Japanese and U.S. baseball. Most major-league players have paid their dues at the bottom of the pecking order and have survived some fierce competition. I'm sure there are some who are the elite from the beginning and don't have to struggle at the bottom, but most players are the survivors. Players who've climbed up to the majors experience a different level of baseball as they move up and go through tough times. And everyone respects those players who've clawed their way to the top like that. Unrelated to age or experience, players have a lot of respect for each other, and praise each other. They respect each other because they know very well how tough it was to reach the top. And precisely because players can deeply respect each other, their play and ability rises to a comparable level.

You yourself are one of those who's climbed to the top, aren't you. You were a fourth-round draft pick, relatively low in Japan, and, after signing with the team, began your career in the minors.

Looking back on it, it was an invaluable experience.

Isn't there some remedy to change the overly slack atmosphere in Japan?

It's really hard to change players' attitudes. You can't just expect to make a clean sweep of things. It might be a better approach to change the attitudes of the younger generation coming up in baseball.

That's quite a harsh opinion.

It's directed at myself, too. But you've got to be strict or else you'll just keep on falling. Say you're not feeling well and can only play at 50 percent. Still you've got to give 100 percent of that 50 percent. You do that and you'll start to see the light. It's hard to give every ounce of strength you have. It's painful, and you feel like you're going to collapse. But if you stop trying, that's the end. You're no longer qualified to call yourself a pro.

That's just like the players who've clambered their way up to the majors.

That's right. What I said might sound kind of overblown,

but it's something I've found out myself the hard way. In the past I've had days where I don't feel in the best of shape and I think, "OK, today I'll take it easy." There were times when I took the easy way out. But for a player like me it was obvious that I'd fall apart if I continued that way. If I don't claw my way up I won't be able to play the kind of baseball I want to play. And I came to realize that.

You refused to run away from it.

It's not a pretty sight when you're struggling. You don't want other players and the fans to see you that way. But if you don't lay that out for all to see and keep on struggling upwards, the next door will never open for you.

Despite these struggles you were able to maintain such a high batting average because there was an inner struggle going on. The extraordinary amount of practice you imposed on yourself was in order to win over yourself.

But I never, ever thought I was practicing a lot.

You mean because baseball was all you ever thought about.

Before I got married baseball *was* all I thought about, 24/7. When I'd get back to the Orix dorm from the ball field I'd be thinking about what I should do to hit better. This made things really hard. After I got married and started living with my wife, though, I don't bring baseball back home. In the car on the way home I'm able now to clear my mind. My wife, Yumiko, helps me put that all aside and think of other things.

I'm sure a lot of fans really feel the enthusiasm you have for the game.

I wonder. There's a part of me that hopes they understand that, another part of me that thinks that's just my own selfish way of thinking. But I did want the fans to understand this. What you struggle over might be different, but everybody runs into a wall someday. And it makes you happy when people think you're really trying your best. Being a baseball player's the kind of job where a lot of people support you, and because of that it's a profession where you can have a lot of influence. Which is why it's not the kind of environment where you can slack off. For myself, though, I love baseball, and don't often think of it as a job.

As you play for the Mariners this season there may start to be a lot of Japanese players, not just ones playing professionally now, but younger players, too, who will begin aiming at the majors. I think that's a wonderful thing, but some critics have said that "at this rate Japanese professional baseball might become a minor league for the U.S. majors." How do you feel about this?

To be able to take your place alongside the best in the world is a worthy thing to do. Even if there's a possibility that Japanese pro teams will find themselves in the position of being minor-league teams to the majors, and even if so many players leave to play in the majors that it becomes an issue, I think that'll be just a temporary problem. As players experience the majors their play should get remarkably more interesting to watch. The techniques players acquire in the majors will eventually find their way back to Japanese pro baseball. If things start to flow that way I don't think it's such a bad thing.

If you take a long-range view of things, there's nothing negative about it.

Playing in the majors may help improve players' attitudes, too.

I expect so. If things stay the way they are, Japanese baseball will keep on running up against a wall. Things will just stagnate. But if a lot of Japanese players come to the majors, while it may temporarily depress the situation, in the long run things will turn around, and it'll prove to be a shot in the arm for baseball in Japan.

Is that feeling one of the reasons why you've decided to take up the challenge of playing in the majors?

That's not the whole reason, but it isn't irrelevant, either.

CHAPTER FOUR

THE DECISION

Two Conversations and an Injury

On October 12, 2000, when you announced that you would use the posting system to switch over to the majors, I felt an excitement I can't really put into words, but at the same time I was thinking that something must have suddenly changed for you. I thought this because in an interview after the '99 season finished you very firmly made the following point: "Though I still have a desire to try to play in the majors, I have to give up on going there any time soon. This can only happen after I become a free agent after the 2001 season is over." But actually your switch to the majors came about a year earlier than this, at the end of the 2000 season. Was there some major change at this time?

There was. It was a completely unexpected development as far as I was concerned. Which is what made it possible for me to join the majors through the posting system before I became a free agent.

Could you tell us the whole process you went through? First of all, to back up a little, was it true what you said in August of '99, that you'd made a definite decision not to go to the majors during the off-season?

I'd completely given up the idea of going to the majors during the '99 off-season. Ever since around '96 I'd been telling my ball club I wanted to go to the majors, but in '99 that desire became much stronger than ever. To tell the truth I felt it was like if I'm going to go now's the time. But it didn't come true.

At that time the posting system had already been introduced, and it was rumored that the first player to be posted under that system would be you.

I thought, myself, that it would be ideal if that could happen. Because as long as I could discuss things with our organization and get my team's consent, then I could go through the required formalities to play in the majors.

But that didn't happen. Did you give up during the '99 off-season as a result of discussions with your ball club?

That had something to do with it, of course, but the main factor was my manager, Mr. Ohgi. I'd been telling the front office for a long time that I wanted to go to the majors, and we'd discussed it a number of times. I was sure that the ball club would make a sincere effort to look into the possibility of my moving over to the majors, and they even told me they wanted to hear my "final decision." In this situation I was expecting that the ball club would be discussing my possible move to the majors with the manager.

But Mr. Ohgi didn't know anything about it. He didn't know how you felt either?

He may have just thought it was an infatuation with the majors. In August of '99, out of the blue, without contacting me beforehand, he showed up one day saying he had something he wanted to talk about.

What did Mr. Ohgi say then?

After I had dinner at one of my favorite restaurants in Kobe, our hometown, he came there by himself and came out with this rapid-fire monologue. He told me, "As long as I'm the manager I won't let you go. . . . I absolutely won't let that happen." He'd heard from the ball club what my feelings were, and was probably also trying to sound out my real intentions, but this was his declaration that no, he wouldn't let me go to the majors.

What did you think at that moment?

It was a shock to hear him say no, but more than that I just listened in silence to what he had to say. Mr. Ohgi said, "Work with me. . . . I absolutely need your power on the team." Once he said this, I felt painfully overwhelmed. In my third year with Orix, while I was still in the minor league, I'd asked him any number of times to bring me up and make me a regular. And he listened to me. Which is why I'm the player I am today. To have someone like Mr. Ohgi, then, say that made things very tough on me, and I felt very apologetic.

So Mr. Ohgi's words to you held you back.

He's the person who raised me up as a ballplayer. So I couldn't very well ignore what he said. I decided I couldn't ignore his wishes and join the majors, so I had to wait until I became a free agent. Also, I really wanted everyone around me to approve of my going to the majors. I couldn't turn my back on the fans who'd always been behind me, cheering me on, or the people in the Orix organization who'd always supported me. In the end the ball club responded that it would be impossible to consider allowing me to leave, and when I heard that I gave up any idea of joining the majors ahead of free agency.

You didn't waver at all?

I'd be lying if I said I didn't. I always find it best to take action when your mind is made up, because you don't know how you'll feel later on. I had no idea how I'd be feeling two or three years down the road. It wasn't even clear to me whether I'd still be a ballplayer in a few years. I wasn't so much uneasy; it was more that I felt the next two years were going to drag out. But those feelings passed. Soon after our spring training camp started in Miyakojima island, in the middle of February of 2000, I was already able to focus on the upcoming pennant race.

After this you never discussed moving to the majors?

It became a topic that was off-limits–for me and for the people around me. I also had some new goals as a member of the Orix team.

You were batting fourth for the first time. And you were also trying to bat .400 that season.

That's right. I had no intention of chasing specific numbers, but I did sense that I might be able to bat close to .400 that season in Japan. So I just naturally became more focused.

So when was it, and how was it, that your move to the majors actually started to fall into place?

It was in 2000, near the end of August. After I injured my right side and had to be on the injured list. That's when things started to get going.

After you were injured?

That's right. After I was told it would take a month to heal and I wasn't able to play ball.

I'd like to ask you again, then, about the path that led to the majors. First, it all began the August 27 game in Green Stadium against the Lotte Marines, your twenty-second meeting of the season. It was the bottom of the third, your second time at bat, and you were struck out by Naoyuki Shimizu, who was pitching for Lotte. Just before that third strike, though, you fouled off a fastball and hurt your right side. The diagnosis was contusions of the oblique muscles. Later reports said that you'd been feeling something wrong from the day before. What exactly was the situation?

That pain didn't just come out of nowhere. I'd felt it two or three days before that. It was the first time I'd ever hurt myself there, so I wasn't sure what to do. I felt a strain in my muscles on August 26, a Saturday, the day after we returned to Kobe from one of our annual road trips to the Hokuriku region. The night before I was planning to work out a bit at the gym in the dorm, but I had a dinner engagement that lasted far into the night so I couldn't go to the gym. If I go a whole day without working out, I start to feel bad, so after I got home I went out running. My apartment in Kobe is near the mountains, and there are a lot of steep slopes around there. In the off-season I run on these slopes as part of my usual workout, but during the season I don't normally run like that. Running like that, the day we got back from a road trip, and so late at night, must have put a strain on my body. The next day, the 26th, I felt a muscle strain on my right side. I thought if I stretched I could work out the kinks, but it didn't work. During the game I felt some slight pain. On the 27th, though, my second time at bat, I really hurt myself. If I had experienced that sort of muscle-strain feeling before, I'm sure I could have avoided the injury. But I never had, so very cautiously I went ahead and went to practice and played in the game. That's the reason I got injured.

There was a sharp pain, then, when you foul-tipped that pitch . . .

It was right when I fouled off a slider. I could still breathe, but it hurt so much I thought, "Darn, I really did it this time."

So the accident happened at the moment of impact.

It was definitely in the part that affects the swing—the right oblique muscles.

Yet in the fourth inning you went out in the field and took your usual position.

A fly ball was hit to right. It was on my right side, so I could field the ball, but I couldn't raise my arm to throw it back. "This is bad," I thought, and I was taken out of the game and went to the hospital right away.

What was the diagnosis?

I had an MRI done and they found inflammation in the muscles. The bones were fine, though.

Did they predict it would be hard for you to return in time for the tail end of the pennant race?

I'd never had an injury in that part of my body before, so I had no idea if the symptoms I was feeling were severe or not. People told me that injuries there take a long time to heal. None of the players who'd had similar injuries told me they'd been able to completely recover in a week or two. They advised me not to get impatient, otherwise that would exacerbate the injury, so I resigned myself to the idea I'd have to get completely well before I could play again.

Before the 2000 season started you went on a new regimen to bulk up, and you were batting fourth, something you'd never done before, so maybe this was too much of a strain on you physically?

I don't think that had anything to do with it. What became painfully clear to me was the need to be very cautious how I spend the days off when we're traveling, and how I should go about training. My condition in the off-season and during the season is different. I have to pay close attention to what my limits are each and every day. That part of the year, after you've gone through the summer, is when I really start to feel the physical strain, so I can't say I was in the best shape, but since that was the season where I really felt I'd mastered the batting techniques I needed, I was naturally confident that in the latter part of the season I'd be able to do better. At any rate, this all resulted from ignoring that initial strain.

At that point your batting average was .387. You were aiming at .400 and now you're out of the lineup, and when they told you you might be put on the disabled list you must have felt terribly frustrated.

Of course it was frustrating. But if I overdid it the injury would take much longer to heal, so it was a decision I had to make as a player, in order to come back as soon as I possibly could. When I think about my physical condition, I think I was actually lucky not to have been batting .400.

You felt lucky?

If I'd been batting .400 and was put on the disabled list people would have thought I did that deliberately to maintain that average. That's the last kind of thing I want to hear. Most likely if I'd been batting .400 I would have gone out and tried to play no matter what. And if I'd done that I would have injured myself so much it might have affected the next season as well.

I'm sure it would have been hard to take if people said you'd run away in order to maintain a .400 average. While you were out of the lineup going through rehabilitation, massage therapy, and taking anti-inflammatories, what was going through your mind?

Recovering from my injury was my top priority, of course, but with all the extra time I now had I was able to talk with lots of people around me. I was fortunate enough to be able to talk with Mr. Ohgi, the manager, and with the president of the baseball team, Mr. Okazoe. Of the two I talked with Mr. Ohgi more, as I recall.

At the beginning of September Mr. Miyauchi, the owner, and Mr. Ino, the club representative, announced that you would not be leaving Orix. You'd given up on joining the majors until you became a free agent, but was there any change in your own attitude?

What led me to be more positive about joining the majors was less something to do with myself than something Mr. Ohgi had said. Soon after I was injured he invited my wife and me out to dinner, and there he said, "It might not be a bad idea for you to think about it [joining the majors]." My wife and I had both been thinking he would tell me again I couldn't go, so that was quite unexpected. Getting Mr. Ohgi's blessing was one absolute condition for me before I could go to the majors, and after this I started to think, "Well, if the manager's OK with it, maybe I should start seriously considering it again."

Why did your manager all of a sudden give you the green light to join the majors?

This might have been just something said over dinner, after all. Because later when I saw him he told me that on second thought maybe I should give up the idea.

So your manager wasn't sure how he felt?

Maybe so. But his first words to me at that dinner definitely did give me a lift. I felt very strongly that, psychologically and physically, now was the time to make the move.

You were able to reconfirm the feelings you'd kept bottled up for a year.

That's right.

After that you continued to hold discussions with your baseball club?

I kept telling them over and over about my desire to move to the majors. They didn't give me a clear go sign, but gradually the ice melted.

During your contract negotiations you turned down the multi-year deal the club proposed and signed a one-year contract. This sent a clear message that you intended to jump to the majors as soon as you got your free agency at the end of the 2001 season. When the club realized that your feelings weren't going to change, then, they ended up choosing the posting system to allow you to go a year ahead of free agency?

I think so. They may have been considering the influence I would have had on those around me, as a player who was definitely going to change teams after the end of the next season.

Influence on those around you? Do you mean that the 2001 season would then be viewed as a countdown to your move to the majors?

That's right. Even if I wasn't consciously aware of it, the fans would view me as a player who'd be leaving the team, and that attitude would spread to my teammates. If that happened it would make it hard to work up the enthusiasm we'd need to play.

People would start viewing each game in terms of how many games you had left to play, not in terms of winning.

Just thinking about that makes me shudder.

When was the final decision made?

The manager gave me the final go-ahead around the end of September. Right after he and the club accepted my proposal, preparations began right away for the move.

What did your wife, Yumiko, say about the decision?

She'd been through the whole process with me, and was as happy as I was about it.

When did she first know about your goal of joining the majors?

I hadn't spoken to anybody about my dream to join the majors until I told her—she was the first. That was when we were still just friends and getting married was the furthest thing from our minds. When I told her I wanted to try playing in the majors, she told me I should choose the path I really believed in. I was planning to go where I wanted to go no matter what other people said, but I guess I did want somebody giving me a push from behind. And she was the one.

Were you happy when she said you should go for it?

I was. Now that I look back on it, I can see that that's what I was hoping she'd say when I told her.

Even before you got married to her, Yumiko was very special to you, wasn't she?

We could talk about everything to each other, even before we knew we would get married—I could open up about everything from baseball to women. We never hid anything from each other. Talking with her helped me keep it all together.

Which is why she was the only one you could consider marrying.

After we got to know each other I'd get her advice on all kinds of things, and I started to realize that she understood everything about me. If it weren't for her there wouldn't be an Ichiro of the Mariners. My wife's the one who helped make my dreams come true.

What a shocking confession.

If I didn't believe those things, then I wouldn't have gotten married, now, would I? (Laughs)

How has Yumiko been after coming to Seattle?

The same as in Japan, keeping very busy. Nothing fazes her. She's a very self-assured person. If she did get worn out by life in America then I'd be worried every time I went on a road trip, and there'd be a lot more psychological pressure on me, but I don't have any of this at all.

She's helping you, instead of the other way around.

You got that right.

Now we come to the press conference on October 12. I was very impressed by what you said then: "I wouldn't be making this move if I thought I could come back to play in Japan if things don't work out."

If I couldn't make that kind of commitment I never would have considered making the move.

You also said, "I have mixed feelings when it comes to the fans in Japan. . ."

I was grateful to them, but at the same I felt apologetic, too, because I'd be leaving Orix and the city of Kobe.

When did you report to your parents about your going to the majors?

Right after the ball club gave its final OK. Ever since I started thinking about joining the majors, in 1996, I've told my father about how I feel. Since I told him that I was ready to go at any time, during those five years my father must have mulled over all sorts of things. Finally he told me, "You only live once. You should go for it." Though I'm sure when my goal became a reality my father had mixed feelings about it.

Did you talk it over with him?

I did. At first he asked, "Why now? If you wait a year you'll be a free agent, so why can't you just be patient until then?" I could understand exactly what he meant, but I told him, "My manager, the ball club, and the company have all given their OK now, and if I stay people will just see this as a preview for

my move to the majors, and I'd hate that." My father just couldn't understand that.

How did your mother feel about your move to the majors?

My mom seemed a little concerned about my health and what I'd be eating, but talking to my wife reassured her, and after that she was upbeat about it and told me to do my best.

A Dream Comes True

October 13 was your final game at Green Stadium in Kobe, then.

I was thinking it'd be a little sad if the stands were empty. So I was happy to see the place packed.

You couldn't bat in the game because you were still in the process of recovering, but you were in the outfield in the ninth inning, and the game ended. After Mr. Ohgi gave a speech to mark the end of the season, and all the players had gone back to the dugout, you came out on the field once again to toss a ball into the stands. On the screen they showed filmed highlights of your career, starting when you first joined the Japanese major-league team Orix, with ballads playing in the background. You got a little misty-eyed.

That music was a mistake. If they'd only played more hip-type music that wouldn't have happened. It was like the final episode of some TV drama. I wanted everyone to be smiling and shouting, "OK, Ichiro—go for it!" but the music messed it up.

You didn't give any showy speech, but I thought the ceremony was very much you. Your final game was then over and you were waiting for the posting at this point, but those days since your injury on August 27 forced you on the injury list were pretty turbulent.

I never could have imagined it in my wildest dreams.

If you hadn't injured your right side and had finished out the season, I wonder what would have happened.

Things probably wouldn't have worked out the way they did. First of all, I wouldn't have had the time to have discussions with my manager and the ball club. And if I hadn't taken action—spurred on by my manager's words to me—to bring about the move, the ball club wouldn't have brought it up on its own.

If you hadn't been injured then your trade would have been postponed more than a year.

That's right. Which is why I see it all as part of the flow of events.

You mean like fate or something?

Yes. I felt very keenly there's a flow of events that's decided somewhere beyond our control. If you don't think that, you just won't be able to make it sometimes, right?

Japanese ballplayers negotiate with the ball club on their own. Of course, recently more players have their lawyer with them when they negotiate salary, but in the major leagues players all have agents who negotiate for them, always looking out for their interests. Were you able to adjust to this system easily?

It's the way they do things in the majors, so I had no problem with it. Having an agent allows you to concentrate on what you do at the ballpark, which makes it very helpful. Having this system in place may be one of the great things about the major leagues.

Your agent is Mr. Tony Attanasio. How did you pick him?

After the end of the season, Mr. Attanasio came to Japan, we met, and I had a good impression of him.

He also represents the pitcher Kazuhiro Sasaki, doesn't he? What was the main thing you were looking at when you made a contract with him?

I look for what the agent's priorities are. Whether he emphasizes money, or what he can do to support the player and give his family peace of mind. I felt that Tony was the second type. I also decided that he had what it takes to negotiate with major-league teams.

Did things go smoothly after you signed a contract?

There weren't any Japanese on the staff at Tony's company. So there was the language barrier to get around, plus a different way of doing business. Talking with him through an interpreter and keeping in touch via faxes was a bit unsettling. But that's all. Everything else went just fine.

After you'd decided on an agent and were waiting to hear about the posting, what was going through your mind? You were the first Japanese player ever to use the posting system to try for the majors, after all.

I thought I could use this formal system to make the move. However, all I could think about was "What if no team picks me?" Of course I was pretty confident that some team would want me, but even so I was concerned about how it would all work out.

I'm surprised those doubts crossed your mind.

They sure did.

Even though the sports papers were filled with names of teams that had announced their interest?

You have to understand I hadn't talked with any of them directly, so I couldn't pin my hopes on that. Information about posting teams is never made public.

November 9 was the deadline for posting and it was reported that fifteen teams had entered bids. Though the names of the teams were kept secret.

That's the time I was most excited. I was touched just by the fact there were teams that had put in bids. I knew I'd be able to continue to play baseball, and that made me very happy.

The highest bid was announced, and the amount announced by Orix, coming from the major leagues via the Japanese baseball commissioner, was a whopping $13,125,000.

It was so much money I couldn't even express my feelings at the time.

Before too long it was announced that the Mariners had gotten the right to negotiate with you. So things worked out exactly as you'd hoped.

They did.

Yumiko, you were the first person to hear from Ichiro that he'd decided to go to the majors, and how did you react the moment you heard it was decided he was going to the Mariners?

Yumiko: I was very happy. I knew how eager he was to play in the majors, and I was happy for him. I think I also knew how important it was that he was able to accomplish this a year earlier than expected, so I was really pleased he could go into the posting system and become a member of the team he wanted to join. Naturally things weren't so easy before this was all decided, but all I wanted was to understand his goals and support him in any way I could. I was also very grateful to all the many people who've encouraged him and supported him all along.

How did you and your husband celebrate?

Yumiko: When he officially made the contract we opened a bottle of wine and toasted each other. Whenever we're happy about something, even something little, we like to have a glass of wine and talk.

You've said from before that you liked the Mariners, and I'm wondering why you were hoping to join that particular team.

A lot of Japan League teams had working relationships with major-league teams. The Mariners happened to have a working relationship with Orix, so even though the Mariners were far away, in another league, it was easy to get updates on them. In '99 I joined their training camp in Arizona, I really respected their players, and the staff of the Mariners was very friendly and open to me, which was a big factor. Also, since I'd be the first Japanese outfielder to play in the U.S. there was bound to be a large contingent of reporters from Japan covering me, and I thought it was important how the Japanese media would be received. It was important that the team be "immune," so to speak, to dealing with Japanese. The pitcher Mac Suzuki [now with the Kansas City Royals] had played for the Mariners, and from this season Sasaki had joined the team, so I figured I could rest easy as far as that was concerned. If the team didn't have any experience with the Japanese media it could cause quite a lot of confusion, I thought. Those are the reasons the Mariners were my first choice.

Like the way you loved the Chunichi Dragons, which belongs to the Central League of Japan, the team of your hometown, Nagoya, when you were little, was there one major-league team you admired most of all?

There wasn't. But I did always like the Mariners' cool uniform, and thought I'd like to wear one.

I can understand that. The uniform looks great on you. Getting back to the contract negotiations, on October 16 Howard Lincoln, CEO of the Mariners, Chuck Armstrong, president of the Mariners, and your agent, Tony Attanasio, all came to Japan and your contract negotiations began. What was that like?

On the first day my wife and I stopped by to say hello. We talked for about thirty minutes, then left, and the rest I left up to my agent.

So you weren't there at the place where they were conducting the negotiations.

No, of course not. Tony and I had already agreed on what we wanted, so all I needed to do was hear how things were progressing.

I heard that it took three days and twenty hours of negotiating before they reached a final agreement. Did it really take that long to settle on the length of your contract and your salary?

I proposed a shorter length—three years—than what they wanted, and that apparently wasn't a problem. It was the salary part of the negotiations that took up a lot of time. This was the first time a major-league team had signed a Japanese position player, and it probably took some time to come to an understanding regarding the amount of money. When a team that gets the rights to a player through the posting system gets to the point of negotiating, there's no other competition as far as other teams are concerned.

In other words, the player is only able to play for the team that has the right to negotiate.

That's right. That's something that players who are planning to use the posting system need to be aware of.

On October 18, then, you finally reached an agreement on the contract, and you were to fly to Seattle ten days later to sign it.

Those were mighty busy days.

There must have been a lot to do, what with moving and getting ready to start your new life in Seattle.

Yumiko: There was. It was just one thing after another, with no time to think, really, with this list of things that had to get done. I'd never been in Seattle, but we had to find a place to live, and moving turned out to be much more trouble than I ever imagined, but I was so busy I didn't have time then to even think about how much trouble it all was. Before I knew it we'd arrived in Seattle and begun our new life.

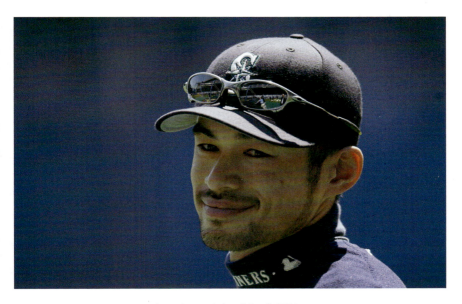

PREVIOUS PAGE: *At spring training, March 2004.* (Photo by Ben VanHouten)

LEFT, TOP: *Receiving first solid food from grandmother Hisa.* (Photo courtesy Nobuyuki Suzuki)

LEFT, BOTTOM: *With father, Nobuyuki Suzuki.* (Photo courtesy Nobuyuki Suzuki)

ABOVE: *At Yankee Stadium in the Bronx, May 2002.* (Photo by Ezra Shaw/Getty Images)

LEFT: *Sliding into second against Boston infielder Nomar Garciaparra.*
(Photo by Ben VanHouten)

ABOVE: *Waiting to bat against Oakland, April 2003.* (Photo by Jed Jacobsohn/Getty Images)

NEXT TWO PAGES: *Racing to second base where former Mariner Alex Rodriguez was waiting.*
(Photos by Ben VanHouten)

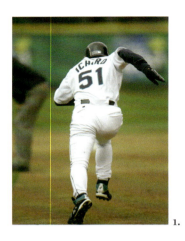

1.

2.

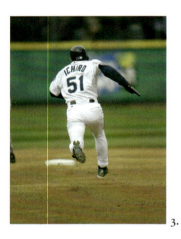

3.

4.

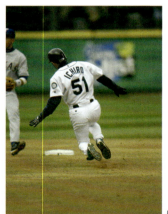

5.

6.

7.

8.

9.

10.

11.

12.

ABOVE: *Congratulating Edgar Martinez on his second home run of the game against the Kansas City Royals, May 2003.* (Photo by Dave Kaup/AFP/Getty Images)

RIGHT: *Returning the ball from right field at Safeco.* (Photos by Ben VanHouten)

1.

2.

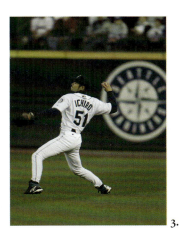

3.

4.

5.

6.

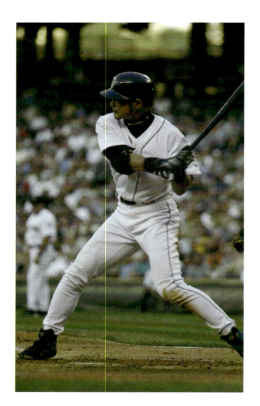
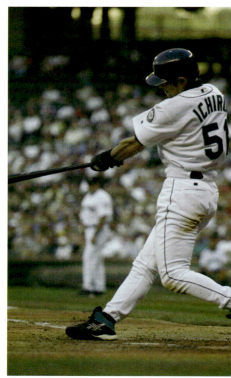

LEFT: *Batting against the Detroit Tigers at Safeco Field, July 2003.* (Photos by Ben VanHouten)

ABOVE: *Diving back to first base on a pickoff attempt during a game with Toronto, August 2003. Carlos Delgado is the first baseman.* (Photo by Otto Greule Jr./Getty Images)

ABOVE: *Pre-game sentiments in Anaheim, June 2001. The Mariners won that day.*
(Photo by Jeff Gross/Allsport)

RIGHT: *Bunting against the Oakland A's at Safeco Field, April 2004.* (Photo by Ben VanHouten)

1.

2.

3.

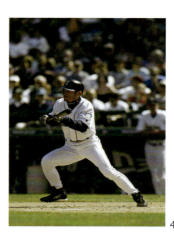

4.

5.

6.

ABOVE: *At a Seattle SuperSonics game against the Indiana Pacers at Key Arena, December 2002, while owner Howard Schultz cheers on his team.*

(Photo by Jeff Reinking/NBAE/Getty Images; ©2002 NBAE)

RIGHT, TOP: *Yumiko and Ichiro in front of Abner Doubleday Field in Cooperstown, New York, during the 2001 off-season.* (Photo courtesy Ichiro Suzuki)

RIGHT, BOTTOM: *"Ikkyu" Suzuki, Christmas 2003.* (Photo courtesy Ichiro Suzuki)

LAST PAGE: *At spring training, 2002.* (Photo by Ben VanHouten)

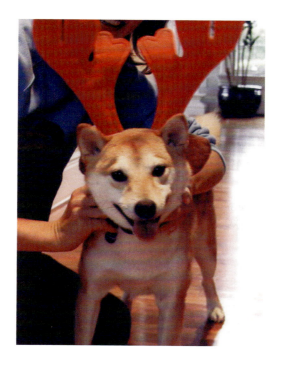

So it was Yumiko who was really the busy one.

Definitely. I was steadily getting over my injury, and wanted to do some practice to check out my condition. every day I made time to train. I had a required medical checkup to join the Mariners, but compared to her I had it easy.

I understand you really wanted to continue practicing.

Since I'd been injured I wanted to get back to my old form as soon as I could. In 1999 I broke my wrist when I was hit by a pitch in a game, and at that time I decided just to rest and not do any practice. When 2000 spring training rolled around I got a little panicky since my body just wasn't responding the way it usually did. It was like my arm wasn't my own and I couldn't throw. I decided I never wanted to go through that again. If I took time I knew I wouldn't have much confidence when we started playing in the spring. I wanted to get back to where I really felt I was 100 percent before taking time off. While the contract negotiations were under way I was trying to get my-self back in shape to be able to play. That was my number-one priority, and by the time we left for Seattle I was back in pretty decent shape.

Signing with Seattle

You and Yumiko flew to Seattle, then, for the contract signing. What was that like?

Howard Lincoln, the Mariners CEO, Chuck Armstrong, the Mariners president, Ted Heid, the Mariners scout and Far East representative, and Hidenori Sueyoshi, who was the interpreter at the occasion, all gathered in the meeting room together, and after they all sat down I signed the contract.

I heard that you were there, too, Yumiko.

Yumiko: Yes, I was. In America typically the husband and wife are together for the contract signing, so I was there since I wanted to follow the American way of doing things.

Did you read over the entire contract?

I did. It was all in English, so I had it explained to me in Japanese.

What sort of provisions did it contain?

Nothing particularly surprising. It was very detailed, however. For instance, so much for housing allowance, or so much for moving expenses. It also listed sports that I'm not allowed to do in the off-season.

So it has very clear-cut restrictions.

That's right. Skiing and snowboarding aren't allowed. And neither are marine sports.

Was there any item at all in the contract that was unexpected?

I was pretty amazed by the "deferred payment" system. That surprised me. This system allows players to collect a certain percentage of their salary for decades after their baseball careers are over. In other words, money they should be paid up front is managed by the ball club, and after the player retires this is paid out to him in installments.

It's a kind of major leaguers' pension, isn't it.

That's right. If you want the money beforehand, though,

they'll pay you the whole amount. I was told most American players want the whole amount paid to them. I opted for the deferred-payment plan.

Do American players use up most of the hefty salaries they receive?

Shigetoshi Hasegawa, who's been playing in the majors for years, told me once that there are some players who don't save anything.

Changing the subject, Americans really like celebrations, don't they? There were all kinds of ceremonies planned to welcome you to Seattle, including the NBA [Seattle] SuperSonics asking you to throw the ceremonial first ball onto the court at the opening game of the 2000–2001 season.

It was very American, but the thought crossed my mind that it might have been a little too much. Of course it was a great feeling to have the Sonics cheering me on. America really knows how to stage events, and get the crowd all excited.

Speaking of which, the press conference to announce your becoming a Mariner on December 1 was exciting itself. You said that you felt like you were in a movie at the time.

The whole situation felt unreal.

Like you were the hero in a movie.

Right.

The commemorative photo that was taken at Safeco Field together with Yumiko was a very American thing to do, too, wasn't it.

The first thing I thought about was to try to fit into the style of doing things here in America. That photo shoot, for instance I was told from the start that it was natural to have the husband and wife together. Ever since I came here I've wanted to adopt a "when in Rome, do as the Romans do" type of attitude and do things the way they're done here.

In Japan it's just not done to bring family members to your place of work.

That's true. In Japan you'd never do something like that, but in America it's expected you'll do things as a couple. If you're not together people might ask you, "Is your wife not feeling well?"

Yumiko, how did you feel about the commemorative photo session?

Yumiko: My simple reaction was that I was very happy to do that. It was a bit embarrassing, but I was very grateful that they'd welcome us to that extent. Ichiro's set records in Japan, but over here he's an unknown player. It made me so happy to see how much they respect him and how much they welcomed us.

Just standing there you could feel that, I imagine.

Yumiko: That's right. Ever since the contract negotiations I could feel how much all the people on the Mariners respected Ichiro for taking on the challenge of playing in the major leagues, and how much they welcomed him. It wasn't the size of the ceremonies so much as that feeling that made me happiest.

At the press conference, Ichiro, you said, "If I'm uneasy about

*anything, it's about what's outside the ballpark," and you seemed
full of confidence.*

The longer I live in this town the more I feel how all the people who love the Mariners have great expectations about how I'm going to perform. I'm the type of person who gets a lot of energy through wanting to respond to these kinds of expectations. The first year I joined Orix, a Japanese newspaper reporter wrote, "If they continue to let Ichiro Suzuki play, someday he's definitely going to be the top batter in the pros." I never met this reporter, and I don't know who he is, but I really felt I wanted to live up to his expectations. It makes me so happy even if there's only one person who feels that way about me, and I always feel it right here [points to chest]. And when I got to be the top batter, the first thing I thought about was that reporter who'd written that article.

*If he reads this, I'm sure he'll be touched. He might even step
forward to announce himself. You moved from Kobe, where you'd
lived for a long time, and now that you're living in Seattle, how do
you like it?*

It's a beautiful city, and I can see Lake Washington from my apartment. It rains a lot in the winter, but other than that the weather is outstanding. The people are very warm. I've heard that the fans at Safeco Field are really well behaved, too.

*Once you started living in Seattle, did you feel any pressure from
living in a foreign country?*

I feel pressure because I can't speak English. I have to be careful about all kinds of unexpected things. Because the mentality and way of doing things is so different. But even if that puts a little pressure on me, I also find it stimulating. It makes you feel alive. A monotonous life without any tension or excitement is something I'll leave for later on in life. I'm prepared for all sorts of trials, but actually I'm finding it more fun than anything else. I want to experience all kinds of things—many different experiences.

This is the first time for you, too, Yumiko, to live in America, isn't it?

Yumiko: Yes, it is.

I'm sure it's much different to visit a place and live there, but how are you finding life in Seattle?

Yumiko: Of course there are some difficulties, the language and differences in ways of doing things, and every day things happen I never could anticipate. I'd be telling a fib if I said it isn't stressful, but more than that, I find all the new experiences I'm going through refreshing. So I don't find it hard.

Doesn't it tire you out at times?

Yumiko: So far I'm fine. We were so busy just before the start of the season, which was a bit nerve-wracking, but I think I'll be able to gradually slow down as time passes.

What do you think about Seattle?

Yumiko: It's a gorgeous city. I love the greenery and the lake, and it's such a calm place. Everyone I've met here has been warm and friendly, which has been a great relief.

How has Ichiro been after moving to America?

Yumiko: He seems really relaxed. I know he must feel some

pressure playing for a major-league team now, but he doesn't have to get worn out being recognized by people like in Japan, so he's much more calm.

In Japan popular baseball players are treated like celebrities. Everywhere Ichiro went people would be screaming and carrying on, wouldn't they?

Yumiko: I'm grateful they pay so much attention to him, but this just added a lot of psychological stress to him. In Japan, for example, when we were in our car, stopped at a red light, people would peer inside, and once they knew it was Ichiro they'd follow us. We tried all kinds of ways not to be recognized, but people would see through it.

I guess athletes are treated differently in the two countries.

Yumiko: That's something I'll learn more about as time goes on, but at least right now he seems to be able to get away from all that stress.

What's Ichiro like at home?

Yumiko: The same as when we were in Japan.

Before he got married I understand he did all his own laundry and cleaning, and even ironed his favorite T-shirts.

Yumiko: I find that hard to picture. Now when he takes off his clothes they just lie there where he put them.

How does Ichiro as a major leaguer strike you? There must be some aspects of him only you know about, as his wife.

Yumiko: At home he hardly ever talks about baseball, but there is one thing that surprised me. When he's lying down sleeping, he'll roll over to the other side, and he keeps changing sides like that over and over. Once I asked him why he does that, and he said, "If you always put your weight on one arm and shoulder your body gets out of balance, so even when I'm sleeping I'm trying to avoid that." That really surprised me to hear that.

So Ichiro is totally focused on baseball.

Yumiko: I'd say so. What always guides him is his physical sense of himself. So whether he's trying to be the top batter for seven years straight or trying to join the majors, if he isn't 100 percent satisfied with his physical sense of himself as a baseball player, he's not content. Even though his batting average is high and he looks like he's at his peak sometimes, his own sense of it is completely different. Usually you think if your performance is bad you get depressed, but if it's good you might get overconfident. He doesn't pay attention to outward stats, but to that physical condition that he's always aiming for, and that's where his confidence lies. Even if people tell him how fantastic he's doing, if he can't attain that physical condition that'll satisfy him, he'll pursue it relentlessly. I think that's where his real strength lies.

Pretty intense, isn't it?

Yumiko: I think he spent twice as much time as other people training to get to the level where he can be confident in his condition.

Is there any particular thing you'd like to say to Ichiro to encourage him now that he'll be playing with the Mariners?

Yumiko: I think he should always keep the same feeling he

had when he first thought about going to the majors. I want him to remember that starting point. Now, when he's attained his dream and will be playing for the major leagues, I'm sure he's feeling all the responsibilities he has to fulfill. People will expect all kinds of things from him and he'll face incredible pressure. I want to tell him you don't have to carry all that burden. When it was first decided he would join the Mariners he wore a Mariners cap all day long around the house, that innocent smile of his on his face. If I could always see that smile that would make me really happy.

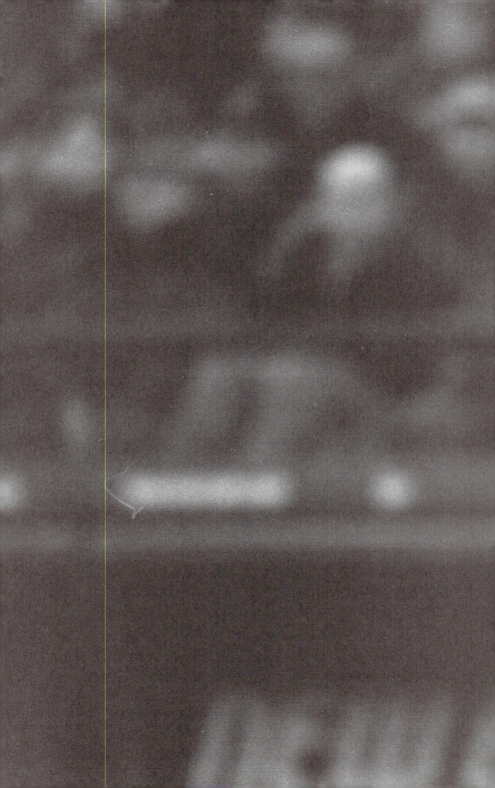

CHAPTER FIVE

ON AND OFF THE FIELD

A Red Glove

How did you start out playing baseball?

My first two or three years I can't remember anything, so I won't be able to answer any questions about that. (Laughs) My earliest memory is when I was three years old. My father gave me a baseball glove and ball. The glove wasn't a toy, but a real glove made of red leather. I was so excited about getting it I carried it everywhere. By the time I was four or five and was going to nursery school I already could use that glove pretty well. Inside the house, even, my father and I played catch and I'd pretend to be batting. Those were my treasures, that glove and that ball.

When did you realize those were part of the equipment used in a sport called baseball?

When I was in nursery school I was always watching the Chunichi Dragons' games, so I knew about baseball. By the time I entered elementary school I understood the rules of the game, because when I was a first grader I'd already joined a Little League team at the Toyoyama Children's Sports Club.

You were already a regular member at age six, weren't you?

You had to be in third grade before they were supposed to let you play, but I managed to talk my way in. I played in the local baseball tournament of Toyoyama. I was the smallest kid on the team so it probably got out that I was underage, but since my ball playing wasn't so bad, nobody told me I couldn't play.

So you made a quite a splash.

I suppose so. At the elementary level I probably stood out. The fifth and sixth graders pitched the ball mighty fast, but I was still able to hit off them.

As an elementary school pupil were you already thinking about growing up to be a professional baseball player?

In a vague sort of way. I didn't just want to be a ballplayer on TV but like the ones I saw live in stadiums. I'd picture myself standing in the Nagoya Stadium. I think I was in third or fourth grade when I started seeing this as my real dream for the future. All the baseball players were like heroes to me. One of the reasons I was so devoted to baseball was because of our local team, the Chunichi Dragons. Three or four times a year my Dad and I would go to the Nagoya Stadium to see them play.

Was this about the time when you and your father began practicing after school?

No, we started practicing together even before I joined the Little League team. The team practiced only on Sundays, but I made a promise to my Dad that I'd practice every single day without fail. I loved baseball so I really enjoyed doing this, and it wasn't hard at all on me to keep my promise. During the four years until I entered junior high school we practiced every single day, one-on-one.

You're right-handed, so why did you start batting left-handed?

I don't really recall, but my father thought left-handed batters had an advantage, so I started batting left-handed.

Was your father a ballplayer, too?

In high school he was on the team, and dreamed of being a

professional ballplayer.

So you practiced every day with your father as your coach. That's pretty unusual.

I was the only kid who'd do something like that.

Your father's said it was like he was just having a good time playing with you every day.

He might say that to other people, but calling it play is sort of glossing over things. It wasn't that at all. He took our practice seriously every day, and did his utmost to help me out, and for me it sometimes was pretty hard to take. After a while it becomes part of your daily routine. For me this meant every day after school going to the neighborhood field, the Iseyama grounds, just down the street from our house, to practice baseball. So it never entered my mind to skip out on it. If I said I didn't want to go, my Dad would say, "You'd better come," and set off ahead of me. Even though I was a kid, when I saw him heading off alone like that I couldn't just sit still. And once I started training again I'd enjoy it. In exchange for my commitment, my Dad made a promise to me, though I imagine it must have been hard balancing it with his work.

What sort of training did the two of you do?

Nothing special, really. We'd jog from our house to the grounds, do some light warm-up exercises, toss the ball around. I'd practice throwing the ball a long way, practice pitching, and tee batting. Then practice batting, with my Dad throwing, and then I'd wind it up by shagging fungoes.

You'd pick up all the balls yourself afterwards?

Of course. And I'd carry all the equipment as well.

There must have been times when it was hard.

I didn't like it when it was cold. My fingers and toes would freeze. My fingers would get so numb I couldn't do up my buttons.

My Father

During practice did you ever rebel against your father?

Yes, I did. I remember, after practice, lying on the grass on the field, not moving no matter how much my father called out to me. After he left, I'd drag myself to my feet, and then deliberately take a roundabout way home, to try to get him to worry.

Was there a reason why you disobeyed?

I don't remember any particular things, but I know our arguments weren't about baseball. I think it was just stuff like he wouldn't buy me a toy I wanted, or let me eat ice cream, things like that. Also I sometimes wanted to stop practice early to go home to watch TV. Those kinds of things. I was a pretty willful child.

How did you two make up afterwards?

I was so stubborn I refused to say anything. And my Dad wouldn't talk to me when I was acting like that. But since we were practicing baseball every day we did have to communicate. I think it was about three months after we began training, I was sulking about something one day when my father started massaging the soles of my feet. That ended up becoming part of our routine, and until I went to live in the team dorm at Meiden High School he did that for me every day. Even if I have my own son someday I'd never be able to do something like that. After I turned pro and started living in the team dorm, I bought an electric massager, which I used. I'd take it with me when we went on road trips.

So when you were an elementary school pupil, then, you were head and shoulders above any others in your baseball skill, and from the beginning your father could recognize how talented you were.

My father told me this later, but he had a classmate from high school who went on to play baseball at the prestigious program at Keio University. He compared me to this classmate. The guy was apparently good enough to have been a professional ballplayer, but my Dad said as an elementary-school pupil I already had more baseball sense than this friend. I don't know about comparing me to a high school student, though. What he meant was the way I could pick up a pitch, my sense of the game, those kinds of things.

Did your father tell you that you had talent as a ballplayer?

Very seldom. He'd occasionally make some offhand comment about it, but that made me so happy, and was a great encouragement.

You continued training one-on-one until you entered junior high, and did you feel this kind of training helped you improve?

Definitely. The more I trained the more I felt the speed of the ball when we played catch was getting too slow. The fungoes he hit to me got too easy, so I asked him to hit them harder, and during batting practice I got him to pitch even harder to me.

There was no comparison, then, between yourself and your other friends on the Little League team.

I'd say so. After all, nobody else practiced the way I did, every day.

I know this isn't the only factor, but didn't those four years of training in elementary school really go a long way to making you the player you are today?

I think so. They gave me what's really most important. More than junior high or high school, those early years instilled in me a physical feel for the game. The feeling of picking up a pitch, of throwing, the feeling of catching a ball. I think it was actually a good thing my father was an amateur and not a professional ballplayer. I didn't get put in a mold, and was able to do things the way I wanted to. It was good because I could figure things out on my own—how to throw the ball faster, for instance, how to hit it farther.

Without that bond between yourself and your father you never would have become a player for Orix, would you?

For the two of us it wasn't anything out of the ordinary, but if you asked me whether I could do what my father did for me, I'd have to say I don't have the confidence that I could.

I understand you imitated the form of some of your favorite baseball players.

That's true. That was at my Dad's suggestion. The pitcher I

imitated was Tatsuo Komatsu of the Chunichi Dragons, and the batter was [Kazunori] Shinozuka of the Tokyo Giants. I learned their form by mimicking them. It was like things I couldn't understand, I'd pick up through imitating them. For example, what's critical about timing. If you imitate the timing of how a batter lifts his leg, it feels different from what you're used to, and if you pick up something there that feels right for you, then you're able to incorporate it into your own style of batting. With pitching form, too, when I pitched like Komatsu did, bringing the ball down sharply, I was able to put a lot behind the pitch, and my own form gradually changed because of this. People tell me now that my batting form is really unusual, but the foundation of this is something I created during this period.

Your father has said that you got some hints from the golf swing of the female pro golfer Ayako Okamoto, who was in the top ranks of the LPGA in 1987.

I only heard about this a lot later. My father's a big fan of Ms. Okamoto. But this does make me feel how much he was thinking about things then.

What you created during these four years, then, you never lost.

I was really blessed with great coaches during junior high and high school who didn't try to force me to correct my form or change the way I played. If your manager in junior high or high school is someone who has his own agenda, he might end up remaking the players to fit some ideal he has, and I'm sure that if I'd played for that kind of team I wouldn't be where I am today.

So you were absolutely confident of your form then?

I wouldn't put it that way, exactly. I just felt comfortable with my batting, so I thought it was OK the way it was. The balls I hit would really take off, and there wasn't anything I needed to change. My pitches had good speed on them, too, so I concluded that my pitching was fine, too.

How did you feel when you joined the junior high team?

I was really looking forward to it. My Dad came every day to watch me practice, all the way through junior high and high school. I felt like nothing had changed, in a way, since he continued to give me advise. And my father and I continued to go to the Airport Batting Center in our neighborhood.

I understand you were pretty famous there.

There were older boys and men there who were seriously into baseball, and I certainly was way above their level. Once I remember batting with the cleanup batter for Chukyo High School, which is a famous school nationwide whose baseball team has won many titles. I wasn't all that impressed by his batting, and I thought, "Maybe I can become a pro someday."

So you felt then that all this practice was paying off.

I could have been mistaken, but I was pretty confident. Anyway, I was taken with the idea that I could turn pro someday. Though if somebody had looked objectively at me then they might not have been very impressed.

But you didn't need anyone else's opinion to come to that conclusion.

That's right. Since I had a very strong sense that my baseball abilities were something I created myself, I didn't care much about other people's opinions.

What sort of vision did you have for yourself when you were in junior high?

There were several famous high schools in my local prefecture, Aichi prefecture, that had strong teams that played at the national championships series in Koshien Stadium, and I wanted to go to one of those schools with a competitive team. I was a pitcher at the time, so I hoped my fastball would catch their eye.

So you threw a good fastball.

In junior high I think I had a decent fastball.

How about schoolwork?

In junior high I did excellent, as far as grades went. I'm quick at picking up things, so even if I wasn't paying attention in class I'd cram for tests and do great. Math and music I got a four on, on a scale of one to five, with the rest all fives. When I went into high school, I couldn't handle both studies and baseball. Studying interfered with baseball, so I didn't study at all.

High School Days

Did you decide on your own to enter Meiden High School, which is affiliated with the Aichi Prefectural Institute of Technology?

I did. By this time I was thinking even more of becoming a pro, so my top priority was being in a place where I could play. It bothered me a bit that I'd have to leave home and live in a dorm, but I figured that might help me get into baseball even more. The baseball field was right in front of the dorm, and we had facilities you wouldn't expect to have in a high school, like an indoor training facility and a weight training room. And also there'd been a lot of professional ballplayers who'd graduated from the school. A lot of the players our manager, Mr. Go Nakamura, had trained went on to careers in pro ball. When Mr. Nakamura first saw me, apparently he said, "How can someone this scrawny play ball?" It's true I was really thin then; no matter how much I ate I couldn't put on any weight. During my three years in high school I drank milk like crazy, and I did get taller, but I still didn't put on any weight.

What do you remember most about your high school days?

I remember what Mr. Nakamura told me when I entered the school: "For the rest of your life you'll never experience anything as tough as what you're going to go through now." My reaction was "Well, we'll see," but once I moved into the baseball team dorm, I found out what he meant. I've never had as tough a time as I did then.

Was it tougher than professional baseball?

There's no comparison. Compared to my high school days, right now I'm in heaven.

What was it that was so tough about those days?

Well, all kinds of things, really. For instance, one of the major jobs for freshmen and sophomores in the dorm was doing the laundry for dozens of senior students as well as for themselves. The problem was there was only a small number of washers and dryers. Naturally the lower students had to do the upper-classmen's laundry. After practice you take a bath, then eat dinner. From then until lights out at eleven we had free time, but everybody spent it washing and drying clothes. But I wanted to use that free time for more practice, and couldn't wait my turn at the washers and dryers—because all my free time would be used up just waiting to use the machines. I hated having to fight with my classmates over who gets to go first. So I started getting up early to do the laundry, but of course there were other people with the same idea and we still had to fight over who goes first. So I started getting up every morning at 3 A.M. I could then take care of all the washing and drying while everyone else was still asleep. Believe me, this wasn't easy. For two years, until I became a third-year student, I never got enough sleep.

You did that so you'd be able to practice between dinner and lights out at eleven.

That's right. The upper classmen used the indoor practice ground, so I'd go over to the tennis ground nearby to practice swinging the bat, or go for a run on the track. All sorts of things.

You really drove yourself.

For me that was just normal. Mentally, it was a lot easier for me than not practicing. What was scary, though, was when the upper classmen got angry at you and made you sit on top of garbage cans in a formal *seiza* style, on your knees with all the weight of your body bearing down on the lower part of your legs. You know one of those round, steel garbage cans about 50 centimeters or so high? We had to sit on top of those, legs tucked up underneath us.

What did you have to do to merit that kind of punishment?

You name it. You have a bad attitude, or didn't rinse the rice properly before you cooked it. Once I remember they caught me eating a soft ice cream cone I'd gone out to buy, and it was up on the garbage can for me.

Didn't you have any problems with this kind of athletic system where the upper classmen take it out on lower classmen?

I guess I occasionally did think it was strange, but the truth of the matter was I was so totally focused on baseball I didn't have time to worry about anything else like that. You just kind of grin and bear it, and accept things as they are. Also, I was really looking forward to what I'd be like after two and a half years of high school baseball. How I'd grow—as a person, and as a player. If after all that very tough training, living in the dorm, the professional leagues didn't pick me up, then I was ready to accept that.

You were able to play in Koshien Stadium in the national high school tournament once in the summer of your second year and once in the spring of your third year of high school. In the latter case you were their ace pitcher. [Such national tournaments are held twice a year, in the spring and the summer, in Koshien Stadium. Preliminary tournaments are held in each prefecture. Fewer than fifty teams of the more than 3,000 high school teams in Japan can advance to Koshien. Ichiro went to Koshien twice, but his team never made it beyond the first round.] For a high school baseball devotee like yourself, that must have really been a special experience.

I definitely wanted to play there once to see what it was like. When I went in the summer of my second year, it was like the upper classmen carried us along, but in my third year, when we went in the spring, we worked really hard to make it there on our own steam.

Was it a different atmosphere?

It was. I didn't like it at all. Maybe because we lost in the first round, but it was just kind of overwhelming to have people looking down on you from those huge grandstands. Koshien is a huge open-air stadium seating 55,000 people. It's the home of the pro league's Hanshin Tigers, and has unique stands down both lines that sweep up in a way that has inspired their nickname: the Alps. Also knowing that it was broadcast live on TV made me tense up. I felt bad because I wasn't able to play up to my potential.

Which brings us to your last summer in high school.

That last summer I was constantly aware of pro scouts. The prefectural championship was the first thing to concentrate on. More than getting to Koshien, to the national tournament, my goal was to get the scouts to take notice in the summer prefectural tournament. The goal I set for myself was, up to the semifinals, to bat a thousand.

Get a hit every time at bat?

That's right. Not to ground out or fly out even once. Up to

the semifinals I hit into an easy out in one game. In seven games I got eighteen hits in twenty-five at bats. In the championship game I went 0 for 3, unfortunately. It was hard losing to Toho High, but I ended up with a batting average of .643. Which I was sure meant I could go on to the pros. Everyone on the team was crying, since we'd done our best but still couldn't win the championship. But I soon got over it.

When you were in your last year of high school, you struck out only three times, didn't you?

I didn't strike out very often, I know that. High school pitchers usually have only a straight pitch and a curve, so I was usually able to make contact. Since the strike zone in high school baseball is pretty wide, the only time I got called out on strikes would be when I was sure it was a ball but the umpire called it a strike. I don't remember ever striking out swinging.

What was your record like in high school as a pitcher?

There were three others better than me. So I left the pitching up to them and concentrated on batting and getting runs for us.

You didn't have such a great attachment to pitching, then?

What happened was, I was in a traffic accident in my second year. I was hit by a car while riding my bike. I got a contusion on my right calf and had to go to school on crutches for a month and a half. Because of that accident I couldn't pitch anymore. After the injury my pitching form was completely gone, and I was assigned to play first base. If it hadn't been for that accident, I'm sure I would have aimed at being a pitcher. After the accident, though, I wasn't able to throw the ball really fast. Tossing the ball from first to second or third is completely different from the way a pitcher throws. While I was playing first, I got used to throwing it the way a fielder does, so when I tried again to throw it like a pitcher, the alignment of my arm was out of whack and I hit myself on the head with the ball before it even left my hand. Anyhow, once you've picked up the wrong form, it's really hard to change back. It was only after I turned pro that I was able to regain my throwing completely. In '95, the year after I got 210 hits, I had confidence in my arm, but I had trouble with throwing it short distances. I'd try to throw it and hit my head. It made me realize how terrible it is when your form goes.

I'm surprised to hear that. But it did work out, because it led to you deciding on being a batter in the pro leagues.

Yes, it did. It was impossible to be a pitcher.

How did you feel about your manager, Mr. Nakamura, after being on his team for three years?

He's the greatest teacher I've ever had. He taught me baseball, of course, but so much more. He taught me how to act when I went out into the world. He taught me a lot of life lessons during our team meetings, saying that you'll only be able to play baseball for a short time, but the real issue is what kind of person you'll be after that. What I remember most are two things he said: "Aim at being a regular in life more than a regular at baseball" and "Strive to surpass your master." In other words, the pupil should aim at becoming even greater than his teacher. All the other team members took down what he said in their notebooks, but I just pretended to write it down. Now that I look back on it, I wish I'd written down every word he told us.

Playing for Orix

We come now to the draft in the fall of '91. Do you remember how you felt when you were picked by Orix as the number-four pick for the team?

From the beginning I didn't have any particular image of Orix at all. I didn't know any of the players, and I'd never been to Kobe. I just thought that I'd be able now to be a professional.

Did you have any doubts about whether you'd be able to cut it in the big leagues?

People might get upset if I say this, but when I watched one of the veterans on the team, Punch Sato, practice, I knew I wouldn't have any problem. He was popular because of his comical behavior in and out of the ballpark. His defense wasn't anything special, and he wasn't a fast runner. I figured that at this rate I should be able to play on a Japanese major-league team.

The scout who discovered you was Mr. Katsutoshi Miwata, wasn't it, who passed away two years ago?

That's right. When I first joined the team, every time he saw me he told me to do sit-ups to build up my abs, and I made sure that I followed his advice. After I made the major-league team he was the only one I could really turn to for advice. He was the only person I could sit across from and really say what's on my mind. He was like another father to me.

I wanted to ask you what you think about the draft system. Things have settled down somewhat with the reverse designation system in place in Japan [the system whereby a limited number of college graduates and nonprofessional players who work for companies can choose what team they want to go on], but some people say this robs you of your right to choose where you'll play.

I think deciding things by lot is kind of fun. And there's freedom to choose in the draft. Of course, if you got chosen and they told you you had to play soccer, that'd be against the law [Laughs]. 'Cause you're still a professional ballplayer. The ones who feel threatened by the draft system are the stars who are the number-one draft picks. People like me who were just hoping to get drafted by some team can't choose which team we can join. For me, the draft was the way I earned the right to call myself a professional ballplayer.

When did you first get the feeling that you were really a professional ballplayer?

When I was in my room at the Seitokan dorm for single players and put on my uniform for the first time. I pestered the older players a lot, asking them how they thought I looked in it.

The manager when you joined Orix was Mr. Shozo Doi. Even after two years you still weren't a regular on the first team, and didn't you find that disappointing?

Not at all. I was only two years out of high school, after all. My aim was to reach that in the third year, which I ended up doing. The one thing I couldn't fathom, though, was being called up to the major-league team all of a sudden, then equally suddenly being sent back to the minor-league team.

Did you and Mr. Doi have a difference of opinion as far as the way you approached the game?

I don't think so, though he could be long-winded, which I had trouble with. (Laughs) In July, several months after I joined the team, I was called up to the major-league team. A miracle, if you consider the situation before I joined the team. A team staffer called my room in the dorm and said, "Tomorrow you're on the big-league roster." But I told him, "It's a little too soon; I'm fine staying on the minor-league team." "Just do it," he said, so I took off from Kobe to Hakata, where the next road series was to be held, to join the team there.

Why did you think it was too soon?

Because I thought I couldn't handle the pitchers at the Japanese major-league level. But in reality I did hit off them, so in my second year I gained the confidence that I could handle things.

But you ended up not being a regular on the major-league team in your second year.

In my second year I went up to the first team three times, and was sent back down three times. Near the end of the season our batting coach told me this: "This is your last chance. If you do what I say, I'll teach you. Otherwise you're on your own." I made it quite clear I wasn't about to listen to him, and the next day I was sent down to the second team. I didn't have the slightest intention of changing my batting form.

What was it that coach wanted to tell you?

What he said was the exact opposite of my fundamental thoughts on batting. At first I followed his advice and from the fall of my first year tried out a way of batting completely different from my own ideas. My idea was to make the change starting in the autumn training camp for young players and by spring training I'd have it down. But it didn't work out at all. I knew it wasn't working, so I never followed his advice again. It wasn't like I ignored what he said from the very beginning. I tried it once, it didn't work, so that was that. The thought struck me that if I tried to adjust my batting to suit the coaches, who may very well change from year to year, there'd be long stretches when I wouldn't be able to really play baseball. There are people who go for the latest-style clothes or change from one famous brand of handbag to another, but I didn't want to change my style, which I was happy with. It's the same sort of thing. If I changed my style to suit a particular coach, then I'd lose sight of what sort of player I was and would fall apart completely. The worst possible pattern a professional player could fall into.

From the coaches' point of view wouldn't you be viewed as a rebel?

I suppose so. Impertinent, for sure. I'd only been out of high school two years, remember. And here you have a guy like me telling the coaches, "No way."

But you had your reasons for saying that.

When I was in high school I never thought about batting

theory or anything. I just went by feel. The first time I ever felt I had a personal style of batting was after I became a professional. Mr. Kenichiro Kawamura, coach for the minor-league team, picked up on my special characteristics right away and stayed with me all the way. Because he was with the minor-league team, I didn't mind so much being sent back down. What he did was give me some very smart advice about the mental aspect of batting. I'd just been relying on feeling, but he's the one who put that feeling into words. He'd say things like "When you're trying to pick up the path of the ball coming toward you, pick it up first as a line, then as a point." I'd never really thought about things like that before.

If you became a coach yourself, how would you teach players?

I'm not up to being a coach. If I did become one, though, I think I'd really let the players have it. I'd probably wonder, "Why can't you do that?" Coaches don't need to be liked by their players, but they do have to be able to explain things so the players are convinced. I wonder if I'd be able to do it. It's hard to say.

Did the system change in '94 when Mr. Akira Ohgi became the manager?

Completely. Things were much more relaxed, the players much more lively; you knew if you gave it your all you'd get to play. I first met him when he came to Hawaii to watch the winter league. I was playing in the league with Mr. [So] Taguchi, Mr. [Masahiko] Kaneda, and Mr. [Hirofumi] Ogawa, all from Orix. I wanted Mr. Ohgi to sit up and take notice of me, so I did my best to try to get some hits.

What did you think of him when you first met him?

He had on white patent leather shoes, white trousers, a white belt, gold sunglasses, and at the checkout register he whipped out this half-inch-thick wad of dollar bills. At first I was bowled over. I was the youngest player, so I did my best to be courteous to him—pour drinks for him at meals and so on.

If you had to sum him up in a word, what would say?

He's the manager. The kind of person who has what it takes to be a manager.

What's your image of what it takes to be a manager?

You have to be able to sit still in the dugout during the game. I don't care what goes on behind the scenes, but in the dugout, no matter what's happening, you have to remain calm. That's what makes a great manager. Right now in Japan, managers like Mr. Ohgi are few and far between. Many managers, while the game's in full swing, get excited all of a sudden when things go well or get sullen and yell when things go bad. Some of them—when the other team ties the game—even get all teary-eyed. If the opposing team's manager is like that, then we've got it made.

How about the use of your first name, spelled out in katakana, as your official playing name? What did you honestly think about that?

I thought Mr. Ohgi was just joking around when he suggested I go by my first name, so I was pretty surprised when he actually followed through with it. He also did that with another player, Kazuhiro Sato, dubbing him "Punch," after his trademark punch-perm-style hair. I thought he'd gone a little too far, but I was happy that the manager had cared that much about me to try and make me stand out. I've got to admit, though, that it embarrassed me when the public address announcers announced the starting lineup with me as "Ichiro," not as "Suzuki," and there was a great stir among the crowd. By the time we'd made one round of all six stadiums that are the home grounds of the Pacific League teams, I was pretty much used to it.

Soon after this your assault on the record books began. How did you feel as you forged ahead trying to hit an unprecedented 200 hits in one season? [In Japanese pro baseball leagues, the number of games played a year by each team in the regular season was 130 at that time. Now it's 140.]

First of all, since it was my first experience, I just thought I'd give it everything I had. I wanted to test my limits—physical and emotional. Not in terms of technique, but to know what it meant to struggle through a whole season, 130 games.

Were you surprised yourself at the number of hits? Or did you think it was just a natural outcome?

I don't know about natural or not, but I did have one huge advantage. The opposing batteries didn't have any data on me while I was on the second team. So they had to feel their way as they pitched to me. And those kind of tentative pitches are very easy to hit.

So you were consciously thinking of getting 200 hits.

When I look back on it now I'm amazed at what I did, but I calculated out how I could reach 200. In May or June I calculated how many games were left and how many hits I'd need, and said I was aiming at hitting 200. I didn't really know much about it being a new record; I was just speaking my mind. I knew that I could reach my goal if I got at least five hits every three games, and that's what I did. Completely fearless, I guess.

Did Mr. [Hiromasa] Arai, the batting coach who joined the team the same time as Mr. Ohgi, give you any advice?

He just let me go out there and hit, without worrying about anything else. He told me, "As long as you're getting the hits, that's fine." He also said that with things going as well as they were, my batting was perfect.

There were also great expectations that you'd bat .400.

I didn't think that I'd wind up batting .400 for the season. I just wanted to show that, even for a short period of time, I could reach .400. Newspapers reporters urged me to go for it, and I decided to try.

Eventually you reached the 200-hit mark, and extended the record even further.

There was a period when I felt the burden of everyone's expectations and I was chasing those stats. That time was really tough on me. Which is why I swore to myself that I'd keep on getting hits so I could clear that hurdle. If you had only one game left and had to get one or two hits, that would be awful, right? I think that's the reason I could extend the record. This doesn't happen to me very often, but at that time I felt some power beyond just myself, sort of a divine force.

The media went after you in full force.

I'd always kept in the background up till then, so I was overwhelmed as one after another they came after me. I was happy about it, but the truth is it was a little scary with all kinds of people popping up. After the '94 season ended I couldn't go out for a stroll anytime I wanted like before.

The Japan Series Championship

From the following year, 1995, you were well known not just on the Orix team but in all of Japanese baseball. Did your attitude change compared to the previous year?

Playing in the pennant race in '94 made me feel like I could start to do things at my own pace and understand my role on the team better. So in '95 I could take a broader view of things. Also, in January of that year there was the big earthquake in the Kansai area, which was a major event.

Where were you when the earthquake struck?

I was asleep in the dorm. There was this loud bang and everything started swaying so much I couldn't even stand up, and I just lay there with the covers pulled up around me. I really felt like I might get killed. I can't put into words how frightening it was. My room was on the fourth floor of the dorm, and I was afraid the floor was going to give out. My stereo speakers and TV toppled over. Fortunately the only damage was some cracks in the wall of the dorm, but the town of Kobe I was used to walking around was destroyed.

Ninety-five was the year for reconstruction in Kobe, so I bet you all came together in order to win the pennant.

There were lots of fans who'd suffered during the earthquake, yet still came to see us play. They'd gone through so much and you'd think baseball wasn't much of a priority, but they still came to cheer us on. That encouraged us a lot, and we did our best to live up to their expectations.

After you set this major record in '94, you went through a lot of changes. For instance, you switched from batting first to batting third, and the other teams were formulating strategies to deal with you, I'm sure.

Actually it was very tough to bat third. Batting leadoff was the perfect spot for me. I could totally focus on hitting when I was first. It feels great to be the leadoff batter and get a hit. Batting third, it's a completely different feeling you get standing there in the batter's box. So what I ended up doing then was going back to batting first. My batting average had gone way down, too, and I was really doing poorly.

So subtle emotional changes affected your performance.

Well, nowadays it doesn't matter where I am in the lineup; I just go out and bat the way I want to.

As your opponents tried to deal with you, you started getting more walks and balls thrown at you.

Walks I expected, but the idea of getting hit by a pitch made it hard for me to step up and bat the way I wanted to. I'd been standing pretty far up in the batter's box, so it's understandable, maybe, that they'd try and brush me back more. Also, I'm the type that, the more I get hit, the more I step up to it.

Didn't you worry that your batting average would suffer?

Not at all.

But if you're walked then you have one less chance to hit. Didn't this mess up the calculations you'd done in '94 about getting five hits every three games?

Once we started the '95 season I didn't count hits that way. The reality of it was that the only chance I got to get 200 hits was in '94.

Certainly a great batting average wasn't the only thing the fans were looking to you for. The showdowns between you and Mr. Hideki Irabu, pitcher for the Chiba Lotte Marines, were quite a hot topic, weren't they?

Yes, they were. Irabu was a formidable opponent. And I'm sure it was the same for him. You could tell that from the way he pitched to me. In the whole stadium you could tell that something was different between the two of us. Which is why it was so interesting when we faced off against each other. Even when he got me out I still felt good about that at bat.

Even when he brought your hitting streak to an end, you still had some nice things to say later on about his pitching.

His pitches were simply amazing then. I could understand why I struck out. What I mean is, I could understand because I gave it everything I had, without holding back. It was like we were kids. Feeling like I'm gonna hit his fastball no matter what—or [him feeling] no way I'm gonna let him get a hit off me. That sort of feeling—neither of us wanting to lose out to the other guy. I never asked him directly about it, but that message came through loud and clear. And I think the fans really enjoyed that. Both the game and the confrontation between me and Irabu.

His straight pitches were something else.

There's no comparison with any other pitcher. At that time he was already at a super-major-league level. Nomo's forkball was fantastic, but Irabu had a curve and a changeup, and what you'd call a slow curve. On top of this he had a fast forkball. Say you hit his best pitch. If you don't get a good piece of it and foul it off, you can feel the shock all the way down to your waist. That's how amazing his pitches were.

Is there a difference, then, between the speed the speed gun records and how fast the ball feels to you when you're actually batting?

Some 94-mile-per-hour pitches seem easy; others seem tough. There are some pitchers who throw it that fast that you're not afraid of at all. Anyway, Irabu's pitches had a power behind them that went beyond just speed. Still, the balls at the Airport Batting Center back in my hometown were slightly faster. (Laughs)

What did you think when Irabu announced he was going to the majors?

If he kept throwing the kind of pitches he threw to me, then I knew he'd have no problem. He was so fast I got the feeling that after he starting playing in America he slowed down a bit.

In '95 you apparently started thinking about winning the championship quite early in the season.

We were overpowering the Seibu Lions, so I knew we had a chance. Whenever we played Seibu we'd go on the offensive first, and score by the second or third inning. Every time we beat them it was by a wide margin, and I think that destroyed their confidence. The funny thing was, when Orix dropped five games in a row Seibu did exactly the same, so I knew luck was completely on our side. The team was able to concentrate on racking up the wins without worrying about anything. That's not an easy task, because even when you're winning you can get distracted and afraid, and fall apart.

When you needed one more win to clinch the pennant Orix dropped four games in a row and didn't seem to be able to put it away. Is that the fear of winning you were talking about?

Maybe we were just too nice, or too weak. It shows you how hard it is when people expect things of you. Our final series at home, in Kobe, was against Lotte, a team we've always had trouble against. Which made us shrink back even more. I remember it well, how they brought three great pitchers one after another. Irabu, Satoru Komiyama, now with the New York Mets, and John Hillman, pitchers you had to admit were fantastic, despite their being on the other side. Orix's pitcher was our oldest one, Yoshinori Sato, who had good stuff that day, and just when I thought maybe we could pull it out, Hayashi of Lotte homered and that was that. Our whole team was in a blue funk, nobody saying a word.

That final win you needed to clinch the pennant was a long time in coming.

I doubt any other team made it feel so out of reach for so long. I felt terrible when we couldn't clinch it at home in Kobe. Nobody booed us or anything, but you could hear this huge sigh come up from the whole stadium. It was really tough to see how discouraged the fans were.

Finally you clinched the pennant at Tokorozawa against Seibu, in an 8-to-2 rout. Orix ended up nineteen and four against Seibu for the season.

Whenever we played Seibu we were unbelievably strong. Now when I think about it, though, we should have clinched it in Kobe. You have to win it at home.

How did you feel the moment you won the pennant?

There are all kinds of wins. There's the type where you're so far ahead you know you'll win, the type where the other team stumbles and you pull out a win. The feeling of accomplishment you get between the two is quite different. I'd have to say we were lucky to win in '95. Of course I was happy, but not really satisfied. And the same thing goes for our victory in '96.

When Orix won the Japan Series in '96, then, you weren't satisfied with that?

People said, "Now that you're the best in Japan you can't top that, can you?" but that's not true. At least as far as our championship was concerned. There were tons of areas where we had to improve. In fact, it felt like there was more we needed to do than ever before.

In the '95 Japan Series against the Yakult Swallows they say that Yakult had a strategy to counteract your batting, implementing a

174

data-driven approach. Did you feel yourself that you fell victim to the strategy of attacking you with inside pitches that their manager, Katsuya Nomura, and catcher, Atsuya Furuta, came up with?

As far as the types of pitches they threw against me, it does seem that they had done their homework. I didn't get much information on that, and it does bother me to hear something like that. I didn't feel like they got me out because they had more data on me, but if that's true I should have been able to prove it by getting hits. I did my best but couldn't. So I don't have the right to say anything. When we lost the Series one to four it was such a shock that all those happy feelings we had winning the pennant just flew out the window.

What was your impression of Yakult?

I thought they were a strong team then. Each player's role seemed really set, and they were a close knit team.

How about their catcher, Furuta?

Batters always are battling against both the pitcher and the catcher, so of course my image of Furuta came into play. Furuta has a fantastic catching technique, and can turn balls into strikes. Umpires are aware of this, and sometimes they'll call a strike a ball because of it. I could sense this happening when we played them in the Japan Series.

Is it true that catchers talk a lot?

Yes, they do. Toshihiro Noguchi, who catches for the Nippon Ham Fighters, praises the batter, saying things like "You're really hot today" or "You the man!" I answer him back, saying something like, "You got that right!" All the catchers now seem easy to play against. After many years in the Pacific League of Japan I've finally figured out how they're trying to outsmart me.

In '96, the year after Orix failed to win the Japan Series, your batting seemed to evolve to another level. You had quite a few multi-hit games, and seemed to be able to hang on and get hits off pitches on the inside of the plate. Did the regrets you had about the '95 season spur you on?

Of course I had regrets, and the truth is I couldn't figure out my own batting and stood there in a kind of daze in the batter's box. I was trying to go after every single pitch.

From the start of the season, then, were you thinking about the championship, aiming at that?

In the spring I wasn't thinking of anything like that at all. In the summer, there was one game in particular that was like a marker, and after that game it was like the team was on a roll. As if the team had closed ranks behind a common goal. After that we finally started to really feel that the championship was a doable goal.

This was when you were already counting the number of games left in the season?

That's right. Before this we didn't really have the championship on our minds much. Orix, after all, wasn't the strongest team out there. A strong team would set their sights on the championship from day one of the season. And their style of play would show that they were aiming to win the championship. We had a sort of neither-here-nor-there type of attitude, thinking, "Well, if we keep this up, who knows but we might win." It was in the latter half of the season that we started to really get going—when we saw the goal out there in front of us—so you couldn't call us a truly strong team.

But you ended up playing the Tokyo Giants in the Japan Series and coming out the top team in Japan.

Even though we were the top team, I wouldn't call it a complete victory. As far as I'm concerned, in terms of the way we felt about it and the way we played, we didn't live up to that title. I could see way more areas we had to improve on.

When it's the Giants you're playing against, do your feelings change—you're more up for the game, or feel like there's no way you want to lose?

I think so. It's a completely different atmosphere when you're playing the Giants. It's like there's an authority that comes with them. First of all, we're much more in the spotlight than before. The upbeat feeling makes you want to try even more.

In the tenth inning of the first game you hit that fantastic home run off Hirofumi Kono, the Giants pitcher.

I felt so much stress up to that point. I just couldn't hit. When I went into the batter's box I told myself I needed to get a hit in this last chance at bat so I could get something going in the next game. It's a long series, I told myself, and you have to be ready to play all seven games. So I wasn't trying to hit a home run. The count ran to 3 and 1, and I was positive the next pitch would be outside. I had this mental image of this straight, outside ball, but the second it left the pitcher's hand I saw it was coming high and down the middle. I made an instantaneous adjustment.

And the timing that adjustment gave you turned it into a home run.

Right. I wasn't going for a home run.

What did you think of the Giants as a team when you played them?

It seems like there are a lot of flashy, showy players, but nobody who's the sort of craftsman other pros would admire. In that Series, though, I did have one regret. I got a hit in front of the center fielder and thought I could turn it into a double but couldn't. I really regret that.

Orix ended up with a record of four wins to one loss.

We did seem to beat the Giants more easily than expected. Before the Japan Series there was a whole lot of information coming in about the Giants. Reports about them every day on TV, detailed articles on the team in the sports newspapers, which made us start to think that with all that info we could win. The Giants players, in contrast, knew next to nothing about Orix. In that sense the Giants' fame worked to our advantage.

In the '97 and '98 seasons people were expecting Orix to win the championship again, and at the same time there was a lot of attention to your setting a new record as top batter. Wasn't there a lot of pressure on you?

The most important thing was the team winning, but the players couldn't keep their morale up for a third championship in a row. That was really a shame. We weren't able to build on all the experience we got in '95 and '96. In that kind of atmosphere I knew I had to do well as a batter, but it was really tough to get myself up and keep myself motivated. Somehow, though, I was able to keep my motivation level up and do well batting. That's what made me able to keep the batting crown.

Just like you did when you were little, there are a lot of kids who've started watching and playing baseball because they're fans of yours. Does that encourage you? Or is it more a burden?

The expectations that are put on me are what motivate me to perform. Up till now most of the time I do things to please myself, but I've also started to feel the expectations of people around me as giving me the strength to push myself to the limits of what I can do. When I take my uniform off I'm back to being Ichiro Suzuki, but once I put on that number 51 I feel I'm Ichiro, the professional ballplayer, and that's how I act.

Reporters

There are rumors that you dislike the Japanese media. Is that true?

I can't generalize about the media. There are some people in it I like, some I don't. I'm a professional ballplayer, people in the media are professionals, too, and we're connected through our work. Some people at work you can open up to, have a heart-to-heart talk with, others you can't. It's something like that, I suppose. The exception would be reporters who don't even say thanks after an interview.

You seem to be more cautious than before in interviews and when making public comments.

It's only natural that newspapers and magazines come up

with attention-grabbing headlines, but there are some articles that distort the truth. I've experienced that. If the person who reads one of those untrue articles is a friend of mine I can give him the real story, but some people don't get the Pacific League games on TV, or live near a ballpark, and all they know about Ichiro the player is what they read in those articles. There's not a whole lot you can do when people who get their information through the print media swallow it whole. So those who put out the information have to be extra cautious.

Which explains why you've become somewhat close-lipped.

That's right. Not all the time, of course, but there are many times I see the printed word as a deadly weapon.

But there are some reporters or sportswriters you can get along with, people you can open up to.

Sure there are. What I can sense is whether a reporter covering baseball is enjoying what he's doing so much it's less a job than a hobby, or whether he's doing it because that just happens to be the assignment the company gave him. People who enjoy what they do and are up front about their feelings are the ones who get through to me.

There are also people who are just the opposite, right, whom you can't trust?

There was one incident that made me really distance myself from the media. Several years ago a monthly magazine published a diary that had supposedly been written by me. But I knew nothing about what was written in that article. I didn't write any of it, but it had my name on it as if I had written it, and had some comments in it about wanting to play in Major League Baseball that seemed real enough. On top of it all, the writer was someone I knew and trusted. How are we supposed to understand this? What could the person who wrote it, and the person who allowed it to be published, be thinking? It's really too bad, but that incident made me distrust people. Unfortunately, when I meet people from the Japanese media my first reaction is to mistrust them. I don't want to have to do this, but I need time to check people out.

The Japanese media needs to rethink how they do things, don't they?

Anyhow, as a professional I can't let that distract me.

I'd like to ask you, if I could, some more personal questions. First of all, about your hobbies.

I like cars most of all. These days I'm driving a Nissan Cima, and recently I changed the stereo system in it. My car is like sacred ground for me, a place where I can be by myself and forget everything. Where I can enjoy my favorite music on a great sound system.

You don't give people rides in your car much?

Never on the way to the ballpark or on the way home from the park. I'm always alone then. Because this is important time for me to concentrate or, when I'm worn out, just to kick back and relax.

What kind of music do you listen to?

These days mostly Misia, a female Japanese singer. Her lyrics are the best. And rap. That's my older brother's influence. My interest in hip-hop music, too, is mostly from my brother. I first heard it when he used to blast it at home and I thought, "Wow! That's cool!" In high school my brother would edit a tape for me and my father would bring it and I'd listen to it in our dorm.

Your sense of fashion is also hip-hop based, isn't it?

That's right. I hate clothes that are tight fitting. I want to have my own personal style. Right now it's mainly T-shirts and sneakers for me.

I wonder what sort of style you'll wear when you're in your forties or fifties.

I don't know; it's hard to imagine. But I know I won't wear slacks and a polo shirt. Probably I'll be in jeans.

You're not interested in brand-name clothes?

I'm not entirely uninterested. I like Yohji Yamamoto's suits. Dark-colored ones. At contract signings I wear a suit, usually a Yohji Yamamoto. What I don't like is a sort of wishy-washy, nothing style. Like the golf-wear you'd find middle-aged guys wearing in Japan. Nothing young about it. For me it's either loose-fitting hip-hop-type clothes or perfectly tailored suits— one or the other.

A Wonderful Wedding

Now I've just got to ask you about your marriage. You got married to Miss Yumiko Fukushima on December 3, 1999, but when did you decide to get married?

In September or October of 1998, about a year or so after we first started to see each other.

What sort of dates did you go on?

Mostly we'd go out to eat. There are two restaurants I know where we could have a quiet dinner, and we'd go there. Or else we'd go for a drive. Once we went up to Mount Rokko in Kobe to get a view of the city at night, but there were too many people around and we couldn't even get out of the car because we were trying to keep our dates secret.

What made you decide to get married?

I could be myself with her, completely. And she said the same thing. Another big factor was that she got along really well with my parents.

Did the two of you decide together when you'd get married?

Yes. There was the timing of her quitting her job as an announcer at one of the major TV stations in Tokyo to consider, and we talked it over and decided on a date.

Did you go to talk with her parents before you got married?

I went to her parents' house in October of '98 and told them that we were seeing each other with the idea that we would get married.

When did you start planning for your whirlwind wedding ceremony?

We'd decided more than six months before to hold the ceremony at the Riviera Country Club in Los Angeles and made a reservation at the clubhouse. But we didn't tell the people at the country club what kind of a ceremony we were going to hold there until the day before. They understood the situation and were happy to help out. I'm grateful to them.

Why did you keep everything top secret until then?

Of course I wanted to tell everybody beforehand—all those who'd helped me and supported me. But I knew if I did that the media would get after us, and the last thing I wanted was for our wedding to turn into some huge media event. As a professional baseball player I accept the fact that to some extent people want access to my life outside the stadium. But for my wife and me, marriage was such an important decision in our lives that we really wanted to be able to approach it as a shared personal event, the way we feel is appropriate, without any kind of media frenzy. My parents were concerned because they thought we should have a large reception where we could thank all the people who've helped me out over the years, but if we did that we'd have to tell a lot of people in advance about it, and there'd be so many people coming to it. I didn't want an ostentatious ceremony, and finally we were able to convince both sets of parents that this was the way to go. For any fans who might feel disappointed that we didn't have a large reception, my thought was I'd make up for it on the ball field.

Tell me about the wedding ceremony.

We laid out an aisle on the clubhouse terrace, leading to a gazebo with an arch made out of roses. Yumiko was led down the aisle by her father, and then given over to me, in front of the minister. We gave our wedding vows in English, exchanged rings, kissed, then walked together back down the aisle and the ceremony was over. We then moved over to the restaurant for a reception.

Who attended the wedding?

Our two families and four or five friends, no one directly related to baseball.

What sort of outfits did you and Yumiko wear?

I had on a tuxedo, not a white one but more of a beige color. Yumiko wore a dress she'd bought on a trip to Spain, a very simple design.

You must have been excited.

I guess I was a little during the ceremony and the reception, but it was after the party, when we were shaking everybody's hands at the door—standing there in front of all these people who'd helped me so much—when I lost it. I broke down and cried. Everybody looked at me like they couldn't figure out why, of all times, I'm crying now. Without all of them we never would have gotten married. Getting the tuxedo made, buying the rings, getting the country club ready for the ceremony—my friends took care of all of that for me.

It must have been a wonderful experience.

It really was. After it was all over I thought to myself, what a wonderful thing a wedding is.

Starting 2000

So your memorable wedding was over and now you were about to start the 2000 season. The fans were all concerned about the pitch you were hit by, how it might affect you. You'd fractured the ulna of your right wrist, and was it all healed by then?

Yes, it was completely fine.

How did things go at the training camp at Miyakojima [an island near the border with Taiwan]? You'd broken your wrist when you were hit by that pitch on August 24, 1999, in Toyama, against the Nippon Ham Fighters, so it was nearly five months since you'd really played ball.

I took my time, feeling my way through it at first. From August to January I didn't play at all. So I needed time to check out how things felt physically. Never since I began playing baseball in elementary school had I taken so much time off from the game. You take that much time off from baseball and at first when you play again it feels weird. Your body's stiff, your legs and arms are out of sync and it feels pretty strange. I knew before the camp started that it was going to take some time to get back in shape, so I wasn't surprised.

When you were playing what felt strange?

My arm was the worst thing. It was really bad. It didn't feel like my own arm at all, like it was somebody else's. I could only get 10 percent of the power I normally had. So my task at the Miyakojima camp was to build my arm back up, starting from square one. Since this was a brand-new start after undergoing rehabilitation following the fracture, I told myself not to rush things, and I did all my training at my own pace.

How long will it take for that strong throwing arm of yours to come back?

By the time the pennant race rolls around everything will be back to normal, I think. Because I'd figured out the pace at which I'd get my arm back in shape. Anyhow, I told myself there isn't any need to panic. If I messed up my arm, there wouldn't be any reason to play baseball anymore. A player who doesn't rely on a strong throwing arm might feel different, but for someone like me, if I can't enjoy throwing, half the fun of baseball would be lost.

Nothing can replace that great feeling you get when you rocket that ball, right?

You got that right. All I want to avoid is overdoing it, wrecking my arm and not being able to enjoy throwing like that anymore.

How about the strange feeling you got batting?

The first at bat at the camp felt really bad, like it wasn't even me up there. My body just didn't feel right, and swinging the bat felt weird. Usually I spend a lot of time with a batting machine of my own in January, before training, but that year I didn't do it at all. Just some batting off the tee. So no wonder I felt slow. I remember how on the first day of camp the batting-practice pitcher had a lot of trouble when it was my turn to bat. I couldn't adjust the timing of my movement to hit the ball. The pitcher was like "Whoa, what's wrong with you?"

So your batting was in as bad shape as your throwing?

No, it wasn't. I didn't struggle with batting that much. Three or four days and I was back to normal. My hitting sense really improved the first couple of days. And that weird feeling and discomfort just flew away. I don't worry anymore about my batting. I feel very strongly that with this feeling I got in April the year before, that "this is it, now I can bat the way I want to" kind of feeling, that now is the time I'll really be able to show what I can do. Starting in 2000, everything is in place for me to finally become the kind of batter I want to be. The foundation's all set. And from now on I'll be able to really show my stuff. In that sense I feel a little tense, like I'm stepping into unknown territory. And of course I can't just aim at repeating what I've already done.

People would get on your case if you just hit .300 now. Hit .400, though, and you'd be a superman.

That 10 percent difference is the wall that confronts all batters. The sense of that wall bearing down on you, and the willpower to struggle to climb over it, are really just two sides of the same coin. Even when I look back on the previous season, the '99 season, from the beginning of the season to the time when I was hit by a pitch in August and had to go on the injury list, I can see how I fluctuated back and forth between feelings of joy and frustration. It was that swing back and forth between emotional extremes where all my energy's coiled up.

Crafty Pitchers and Calculated Home Runs

In the '99 season was there any particular player who got your pulse racing?

I really had to be on my game when I faced Daisuke

Matsuzaka, the young pitching phenom of the Seibu Lions. Very seldom was the stadium as crowded as it was then. It'd been a long time since I'd felt that much excitement. May 16, a game at the Seibu Dome, was the first time I faced him. Since it was the first time, I decided not to overthink the situation. But he beat me. He was simply amazing—he struck me out three times in a row. To tell the truth, striking out was the last thing I thought I'd do. But his changeup was better than I ever imagined. His pitching form was outstanding, too. When he threw it you could barely catch a glimpse of the team logo on the front of his uniform. Proof that he was keeping everything close to his body, which made it tough to pick up his arm and hand.

In that particular game Matsuzaka threw seven pitches to you that were clocked at over 94 miles per hour. How did the speed of those pitches feel to you?

His pitches straight into the strike zone didn't seem so fast to me. Not that there weren't any, but not the kind of pitches that make you jump up in surprise. His pitches just outside the strike zone, though, had a lot of authority. When I found myself in a pinch, I'd feel like chasing after pitches, even ones that were a little high, a little on the outside, or a little low.

What's the most effective weapon in his arsenal?

I'd have to say his slider. That's the pitch that's really him. The second time I struck out there was nothing I could do. The trajectory of the pitch was completely different from what I visualized. It curved much more than I imagined, and there was nothing I could do. So the third time I struck out I was thinking he'd come more inside, but he threw me completely off.

Was he trying to outsmart you, do you think?

I really don't know. You should try asking him. [Editor's note: Matsuzaka's last pitch was somewhat of a mispitched slider that didn't break and come inside as much as the pitcher intended.]

The fourth time up all five pitches were fastballs. Three of which were clocked at over 95 miles per hour.

The fourth time up I thought for sure I'd get a hit, but it just wouldn't go down right and I ended up walking. Each time I faced him I tried all sorts of things, but wasn't able to get it all figured out, not by any means. There were still all kinds of things I wanted to find out, and to try out. So as soon as it was over I started to think ahead to the next time I faced him.

Did facing him get you all worked up?

Totally. There was a joy to it that went beyond just winning or losing. The kind of thrill you get in a one-on-one confrontation. He's an unbelievable guy. Only eighteen. You almost want to hate him. (Laughs)

But you got your revenge for the three strikeouts when you hit your 100th career home run off him. That was on July 6, at Green Stadium in Kobe.

I homered in my fourth at bat, but the truth is, I thought I had my home run pitch during my third at bat, but missed it.

That was when you popped out foul to the third base side.

My timing was just a bit off. I mishit it. It was exactly the kind of ball I could have hit. Fortunately I got the same kind

Ichiro and former teammate Ruben Sierra.

of pitch in my fourth at bat and I hit it like I'd pictured it.

So your 100th career home run was something you planned to hit?

Of course. When all the pieces fall into place like that, it wouldn't be any fun if you didn't make the most of it. During the season there are very few times when you're given a chance to do things just like you pictured them happening. Also, I'm not the type of batter who can hit a home run very easily unless I aim for it. My hits are mostly the low-trajectory type, so to make it a home run I have to angle it differently. I have to have a mental image of striking the bottom one-third of the ball. One hundred percent of my home runs are ones I was aiming to hit.

So you aim at certain pitches depending on the pitcher?

Sure. Which is exactly why I hit very few home runs my first at bat in a game. I have to get a feel for what the pitcher's doing that day, and analyze my previous at bats against him, and then I can tell myself, "If he throws me this kind of pitch in this spot, I've got a good chance to hit it out." Since everyone expects me to get some hits, it's dangerous for me to go for a home run right from the start. Of course, a home run's even better than a regular hit, but I can't be certain of hitting one the first at bat.

So even with you, you have to go for it if you're going to hit a home run.

That's right. The only time I get a home run without aiming to hit one is when my bat brushes the bottom of the ball and hits it at a different angle from the one I'd been mentally picturing.

Looking at your statistics I notice that almost every year you've gone up in the number of doubles, triples, and home runs you've hit. Have you consciously been trying to hit the ball farther and ended up hitting more home runs?

Doubles and triples aren't something I'm necessarily aiming for. They just happen when you get a hit that gets through the fielders. People might think home runs are just an extension of a regular hit, but that's not the case. A home run is in its own category. I hit home runs when I'm trying to hit them. Though I'm well aware of the fact that I'm not the kind of batter who's able to hit a home run any time he's at bat.

Have you thought about wanting to become a home run batter?

I certainly wouldn't mind hitting more home runs. But if that means getting fewer hits, then that's putting the cart before the horse. I absolutely never want to do that. Because getting hits is the job I've been given to do. . . . Now that you mention it, though, I've actually been getting fewer triples these days. It's gotten a little too tiring to try to run to third, so I don't. My recent doubles are stand-up doubles where I can basically walk on in to second. This kind of attitude isn't good at all.

For most of your career you've batted leadoff, but now in the 2000 season you're batting third in the lineup. Have you had to be more cautious batting third instead of first?

Well, there is that, but there's no doubt there are a few points I have to do some soul searching over. Baseball's all about forging ahead. Forget that and you'll suffer the consequences. One thing is, I'm not going to hold back anymore when it comes to running.

The All-Star Game on July 24, facing the Giants' young crafty pitcher Koji Uehara, you also hit a home run.

In that game I was experimenting.

What do you mean?

In regular-season games I use a tremendous amount of time in batting practice. I'll keep on going till I'm satisfied with my batting. But I wanted to see what would happen in a game that's not part of the regular season if I stepped up into the batter's box without even touching my bat beforehand. So I didn't practice for two days before the game.

And you ended up hitting a home run and a double off of Uehara.

The fact that I could send his forkball over the fence in center field for a home run shows how well I could pick it up. But you do have to prepare for it. I missed a lot of balls completely, and couldn't hit the ball when I was trying to foul it off. My reactions were slow because I'd taken so much time off, and I realized you can't slack off. If you do, you slow down too much.

What did you think of Uehara as a pitcher?

His pitches have authority, but more than that is the way he sets the tempo, no matter where he is or who he's facing. The fielders behind him seem to ride the tempo he sets and they rise to a higher level with him out there. The batter usually ends up hitting what Uehara wants him to hit. I'm sure the rest of his team must feel really good when he's pitching. It's like an aura, I guess you'd say; the whole feeling that surrounds him urges them on to win.

It's like when he's pitching they feel they're invincible.

I agree. He's one of the very few pitchers who's got that sort of power.

I remember being impressed the time Uehara was forced to intentionally walk Roberto Petagine of the Yakult Swallows, who was battling with Uehara's teammate Hideki Matsui for the home run crown, and Uehara wiped away a few tears on the mound at having to do that.

I really admire what a tough competitor he is. No need for tears, though. (Laughs)

All sorts of elements factor into a game at times, don't they?

Our first goal is to make the kind of plays that excite the fans. Everyone's hoping for a great game, and it's plain stupid to shirk that responsibility just because of somebody else's record. In any case, I do admire Uehara's determination.

Hit by a Pitch

As you get toward the end of the pennant race, there is a tendency for people to go all out to set individual records, though.

When you're trying to win the championship you do have to give up intentional walks. Because winning is everything. But the implications are different when you're just playing late-season games that don't really count for anything. The fans who come to see those kinds of games are people who genuinely love baseball. Even if we're out of the pennant race they come to see us. To me it's just plain rude to ignore those fans and discard the real thrill that the game can bring. Continue to do that and nobody will come to the games anymore.

In 1999 you were hit by a pitch, which took you out of the lineup. Did it feel like it was intentional?

That particular at bat I'm not sure. That day I was standing back farther in the batter's box than I usually do. Later I heard that the catcher had set up left of center, away from me. The ball that hit me was a screwball. I think it just got away from the pitcher.

He lost his control, you mean?

It happens sometimes. You know, some hit-by-pitches are just accidental—the pitcher's trying to work you inside and it simply gets away from him—and then there are those that are intentional. Of course the pitcher has his own territory to work in as he tries to get the batter out. But inside the batter's box is the batter's territory. It's perfectly understandable to get angry at a ball that comes into the box and brushes you back. I can understand, though, how some pitches are actually aimed at you. Because sometimes I feel pitches aimed at my waist or buttocks are deliberate.

But dangerous pitches thrown at the head are a problem in Japan.

That's the one thing I refuse to believe happens. I think those are just pitches that get away from the pitcher and happen to come toward your head.

You usually don't show much when you're in pain, even when you're hit by a pitch, but that time you were hit you did wince.

It felt really bad 'cause it hit the part underneath the wrist where there's hardly any flesh. There was this immediate flash of pain and I had the feeling this wasn't just an ordinary injury. Just touching it with the tips of the fingers of my left hand made it ache. The manager yelled to me to take the base, but as good as I am at taking pain I told him to hold on a minute.

You were taken out of the game after that.

I waited a day, just to see how things would go that night, but the next morning it still hurt. So I knew I couldn't play that day. Our team public-relations guy and I took the train from Toyama, where we were playing, back to Osaka.

Thus ending your streak of 763 consecutive games.

Even when I got back to Kobe I was still thinking about the

time. I'd look at my watch and think, "Oh, the game's already started," or "They must have finished the fifth inning by now." When the game was over I really did feel like "Ah, that record's all finished now."

That was a shame, wasn't it?

I'd worked so hard for it. It does make you feel kind of sad when something that's continued so long grinds to a halt. I guess the only good point is that the record wasn't stopped because I'd done something dumb and injured myself. That made me feel better. Up to this point I'd always been hit on the backside of my body and never been badly injured. It would hurt for a day or two and it'd be hard to move, but never an injury that did any terrible damage. I've been hit by quite a few pitches, but I've been lucky, I suppose. There are ways of avoiding it. Players who aren't good at getting out of the way get hit on the front side and suffer some major injuries.

Did they tell you right away that this injury would take a long time to heal?

The place the ball hit me was a very delicate spot, and even after many examinations they couldn't find any fracture or crack. But since it was taking so long to heal they finally diagnosed it as a possible hairline fracture of the ulna. With such complicated symptoms and slow recovery, I had to resign myself to being put on the injured list and going through rehabilitation.

This was just at the final sprint toward the end of the season, wasn't it?

I'd lost weight in the summer, but as far as my batting goes I had one more peak to climb, so I did feel bad about it.

Did you continue training even after the injury?

I did what I could. I'd do strength training for the lower half of my body, and jogging. I went every day to the gym at the Orix dorm. But I could only do a light workout. The following January, just when things had gotten better, I was using one of these machines that test how strong your arms are and I over-did it and messed up my hand again. I thought it'd be OK since I could just use my elbow and not have to bend my wrist, but it put too much pressure on the area around the wrist. That set me back a week in my recovery. After that I took it easy and it healed smoothly.

What was it like being completely away from baseball?

At first it was hard to hold chopsticks or brush my teeth. After a shower I couldn't dry off with a towel. It was pretty tough. But not being able to use a glove or bat actually helped me get over it. I did things I couldn't normally do, and had a lot of fun. I'd go out with friends to the Sannomiya area in Kobe, go to concerts like Peter and Yashiki Takajin. I went out walking around the city every day. I enjoyed that. It was a positive thing for me to be able to see a different world for a while, for a change of pace.

As a practical matter, are there ways for batters to avoid getting hit by a pitch?

The main thing is to get away from it. If you do get hit, you've got to show how tough you are, that it's not going to make your batting average, or the number of hits you get, go down. You've got to make the pitcher know he got away with it once but it didn't help. You've also got to show them how the fans get riled up about pitchers who try to get away with intentional walks or throwing at the batter. That's the only way you can become a batter who doesn't give in to pitches thrown at you. That's the way I see it.

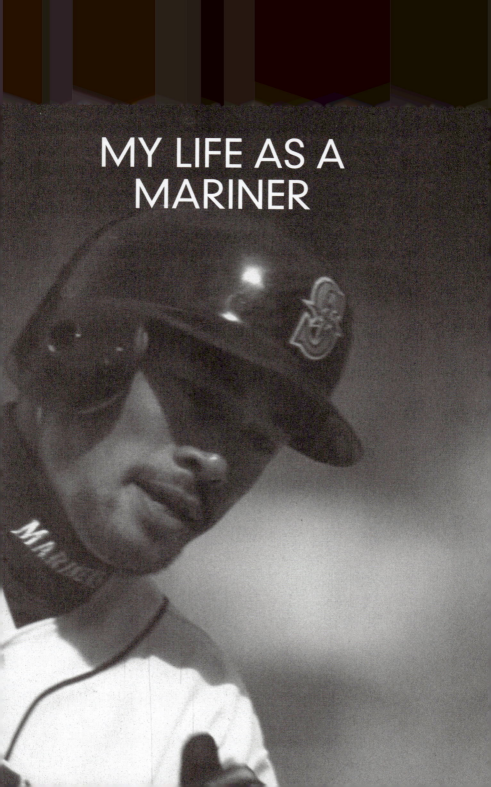

MY LIFE AS A MARINER

American Fans

During these three years you've been playing in the major leagues you've often commented that American fans really know their baseball. When do you get this feeling?

First of all is the reaction of the fans when I hit a sacrifice. The way they applaud me when there are no outs, a runner on second, and I ground the ball to second, allowing the runner to go to third. They know really well that by doing that I've increased our chances of scoring a run. It really makes a big difference to a player whether or not the fans understand this kind of play. Also, when I first started playing in America it surprised me when I let what I thought was a ball go by, the umpire called it a strike, and the fans started booing. I think that shows how much the fans really concentrate on each pitch. Of course, when this happens in Seattle I'm on the home team and the fans are going to be on my side. Even so, they're pretty consistent in how they judge balls and strikes. When I think a pitch is a strike and let it go by they don't boo very much. They do boo, though, when I let what I see as a ball go by and it's a called strike. I was quite surprised by how consistent their reaction is. They watch each play very closely.

One other thing I'm grateful for is how consistent the fans here are in how they judge each play. When you make a good play, they don't raise their expectations for the next play. They know where to draw the line between what's possible and what's not. I'm thankful for that. They want me to play within my abilities and don't have unreasonable expectations.

For instance, when you're in the field and make a great catch and the next time you try to make a diving catch. Even if you don't get it the fans appreciate the effort and applaud.

You get that reaction a lot. That's another thing I'm grateful about.

When fans are watching a game and deciding whether a pitch is a strike or a ball, it's hard, depending on the angle they're watching from, to make it out. You have to be an experienced fan to call it right. The fans really have to be paying attention or else you won't get this sort of "justified" booing.

There's an interesting up-and-down feel to the way fans watch the game here. They concentrate hard on the game, but also make sure they have time to sit back and relax and enjoy a hot dog. As a fan, it's not possible to focus entirely on the game for three straight hours. When they want to relax, they relax. When they want to sit up and focus on the action, that's what they do. They're quiet when there's not much going on in the game, and excited when things really get going. This kind of modulation, the rhythm the fans get into here, is great for the players.

The fans and player are in sync, then.

The players get energized by the fans. That can't happen if they're always cheering the same way throughout the game. This variation in response you see with the fans helps players get into a rhythm. That's definitely one of the special characteristics of major-league fans.

Is that kind of rhythm hard to get into in Japan, then, where from start to finish they're banging drums and blowing trumpets?

That actually creates a kind of barrier between the players and the fans.

I was surprised to see how many fans in the majors keep scorecards during games. Even elderly women.

You see grandfathers with their grandchildren, fathers and kids, and really get the feeling of how the enjoyment of baseball gets handed down from one generation to the next. Even with the same number of fans in a stadium, there's a difference in the quality of the fans in America and Japan. I'm sure there are fans here who aren't too sophisticated, but they seem to be fewer.

Are the fans different in other parts of the country, at different stadiums?

Of course. It's hard for me to say this, but the first time I played in Oakland people threw things out onto the field, while in Texas everything was very peaceful. When you go out east, to places like Boston or New York, there's another kind of intensity that's different from that in Oakland. You get the feeling there are a lot of die-hard baseball fans there. So each region of the country is very different.

How would Seattle fans fit into this?

They're great. They're very well mannered. I was a little surprised, though, when they booed Alex Rodriguez.

You mean Seattle fans booing A-Rod after he moved from the Mariners to the Texas Rangers?

I expected it in the beginning, but they're still doing it. Not so much as in the beginning, though. I found that surprising. I thought after a while they'd stop. Alex got a big ovation at the All-Star Game in Seattle in 2001, so I was expecting the fans wouldn't boo him anymore, but they do. It's died down from what it was in the beginning, but has stayed kind of steady after that.

How do you feel about the new four-year contract you signed with the Mariners on December 18, 2003?

The new contract doesn't necessarily guarantee that I'll be playing in Seattle for the next four years, since the possibility is always there I could be traded. I've had some good stats from 2001 to 2003, but that doesn't guarantee anything about the next four years. I think players who sign big four-year contracts like this can be put into two groups. Players who play baseball so they can have some security in their lives feel really relieved when they sign a long-term contract. Some of them lose the desire to improve their baseball skills and grow as players. The other type of player who gets a multiyear contract feels he's been provided with the security he needs to settle down and devote himself entirely to the game. I'd like to be this second type of player, and I believe I can be. I've heard there have been quite a few players in America who got injured and couldn't play after signing multiyear contracts. I don't want to be like that, and as long as I can enjoy playing ball I hope to keep playing the way I have been. I want to always keep that in mind.

Getting 200 Hits—Three Years in a Row

In the past three years you've had 2,018 at bats and faced 7,716 pitches in the regular season, even more if we add postseason play. In your time in the majors so far, what sort of challenges have you experienced when you're up at bat?

Well, there are two important elements in batting. There's a part of you that needs to be aggressive and a part that needs to be patient. These are contradictory elements, but unless you can be both, there'll be an imbalance in your batting. If one is stronger than the other, say the aggressive part, then you'll chase pitches you don't really want to go after. If the patient part is stronger, you won't go after pitches you could hit. But as long as both these batting fundamentals are working together your batting will be in balance and you'll always be able to do well. Up till now I've been able to keep both these elements under control, but in the second half of the 2003 season—actually, I'd include the 2002 season in this—I started to struggle as I approached the 200 hit mark. As I got closer to the goal, I lost control of that part of batting and sort of lost focus. This experience showed me that figuring out how to keep this under control is a major issue I'm going to have to work on from now on.

In the 2003 season it seemed like you couldn't get up to speed in April (batting .243 for the month), and also starting from the end of August you were in a slump. Was there something qualitatively different between these two periods?

They were totally different. In August I felt kind of agitated, and that affected me physically. In April it was purely a physical issue having to do with the way I was using my body. Not a mental issue.

In Japan, too, you had a lot of slow starts to the season. Was the situation in April here different in any way from that of the start of the season in Japan?

It was. In April 2003 I had too many high expectations for myself. That was the problem. It's a difficult thing—I have this basic sense that in order to maintain my level of play I always have to be improving, but if your desire to improve gets too strong it winds up being counterproductive. There's a balance you have to maintain, a point where I need to stop, a point beyond which I shouldn't push myself. Later on it might be good to push my limits further, but at that point when I tried, everything got out of balance and it affected me physically. That was what April was like.

What is it you were aiming for?

Form, basically. Near the end of the 2002 season I had a great opportunity to learn something about batting, and I wanted to maintain that. I took one element from the batting form I used to have—sort of like pulling it out of the back of a drawer—and added it on to my present form. Just combining good elements, though, doesn't mean things go well. That was the issue I was working through. My condition and emotions change from year to year, and things that worked out in the past don't necessarily work out now. What's most important is the ability to figure out what's best for me right now.

When you say you were working on form, what exactly do you mean?

In Japanese there's an expression, *nimai goshi,* which means doubling the strength in the lower half of your body. That's what I was trying to create. So that when I faced a pitcher, even if my stance collapsed for a moment, I could get it together again. I was consciously trying to do that. But what happened was this led to the imbalance I felt in April, the one I described.

When does your batting form fall apart?

Especially when a left-handed batter faces a left-handed pitcher who throws big breaking curves and sliders, you get this image of the ball coming from behind you and often you pull back for a moment. There are a lot of players who, if they pull back like that, miss their chance to hit. I wanted to be able to get right back in position, ready to go.

Is that an issue of just getting your body back in position, or is there also the mental aspect of having to not back down?

It's a combination of both. Usually I'm OK without even thinking about it, but I started to think too hard and things fell apart a little.

So in the past, when you were in top condition and could track the ball well visually, even if your stance collapsed, you were unconsciously able to hang in there and hit. This time, though, you were trying to do this more on a conscious level?

That's exactly it.

What sort of negative effects did this have?

I use the term "wall," which in the case of a left-handed batter like myself means you're very conscious of this "wall" on your right side. In the batter's box you try really hard not to show the letters on the front of your uniform to the pitcher. I became too conscious of this and found that, when I got set to hit, everything had shifted toward the catcher, even the toes of my left leg. Usually when I'm set, the toes of my left foot face straight forward and my right foot is angled slightly in, but now I was getting set with both feet pointing toward the catcher. If you took a photo of it you could clearly see the difference between this and the way I used to set up. If you're turned in too much like that and have a tough ball to hit, you have to get your body, which is twisted out of position, back to where it should be. It's best to minimize the amount of movement involved, but for me it had gotten too pronounced. Your body shakes a little, of course, which blurs the incoming ball. So I was having a lot of trouble picking up the ball correctly.

Did you notice the negative effects these overly high expectations had on your batting right away?

April is the beginning of the new season, a time when I find myself thinking about all kinds of things. Since we don't play any games during the winter off-season, your sense and feeling for the game don't return for a while. So the batter tries to figure out the reason why he can't get his rhythm back. I didn't think it was an issue with my form, but after playing a few games I noticed something was different about it after all.

It took a while to pinpoint the reason?

That's right. During spring training I still was using the old form and getting hits, so I didn't think that was the cause. That's kind of scary. Eventually I realized what I had changed and thought I should try to get back to the way I had been batting. I wasn't sure if that was the cause, but it was a possibility. I was uncertain about it, and wasn't 100 percent confident about making the change back.

Along with this your bat head speed went up, and with other elements in the mix you were able to hit more kinds of pitches. And your body sort of reacted to this. Did all of these together make it hard for you to get up to speed in April?

So much of the time I feel like I can hit, and I lose the sense of patience you need. I started going for pitches I never should have tried to hit. I lacked patience. That, plus these high expectations I put on myself, were the two main reasons.

What exactly do you do to be patient?

I just had to have a lot of confidence in myself—that's the only way. And then there was the physical aspect I discussed, so I had to correct both at the same time—work on them simultaneously. That balance finally started to mesh well in a game against Chicago when I faced Bartolo Colon.

I imagine that being patient would also make your timing off, too. Did you gradually adjust this, too, as you played more games?

Of course. Even if you understand the problem, though, that doesn't mean you can correct it right away. It's a process of repetition—you experience the negative aspects of being patient, then you charge ahead, then try being patient again. That way you slowly get your batting in balance.

So in this game on May 4, 2003, against the Chicago White Sox, you did a wonderful job of picking up a 98-mile-an-hour fastball of Colon's for a home run. But you've said that you already got the feeling back in the previous at bat.

That's right. I flied out to first that time, but found the way I was picking up fast pitches was different from before. And I thought, this will work. What's different about me is that I don't get input about batting when I get a good hit. It's when I don't that I understand the reason why things turned out the way they did. This is similar to the feeling I got in a certain at bat in the spring of 1999 in Japan. The feeling you get then stays with you for a long time. The feeling batters get when they make a good hit and think, "This is it!" doesn't last for long. You lose it pretty soon.

So in this at bat against Colon did you get a sense of hitting a fastball that went beyond what you've called "picking up the ball visually and hitting it before you actually hit it"?

That feeling came back to me. It wasn't something that went beyond that.

The pitch you fouled out on at first, this pitch by Colon, then, was a kind of turning point?

It was.

I'd like to turn here to a review of the last three years, from 2001 to 2003. In 2001 you left Japan for the U.S. and in that first spring training adjusted your timing. In Japan you were in sync with the "one, two, and three" kind of rhythm of pitchers there. But you found yourself out of sync with the pitchers in the majors with

their faster pace. Before the season began you'd made the adjust-
ment. I think that was a kind of turning point in your batting, too.
Up to this at bat against Colon, did you have any other crucial
turning points like this?

Like I was saying earlier, in the beginning of September 2002,
I seized a wonderful opportunity. I figured out how to relax.

Relax?

Up till then I've always wanted to relax my hands—my arms
and my grip when I hold the bat. I wanted to relax my hands
more when I'm holding the bat, but couldn't, even when I deliberately tried to. When I examined what was going on with
my whole body, I realized I was tensing my knees. I had to get
the tension out of my knees if I wanted to relax my arms.
That's when I understood how the body's put together. That
was a big discovery. And through relaxing the knees I could get
the feeling that the bat's head speed was getting faster.

You relax the tension as you're waiting for the pitch?

Of course when I actually swing the bat I grip it hard. I relax
until just before I start the swing. Up to that point I try to relax as much as I can. If you don't relax you can't show the kind
of burst of power you need.

Did you get this feeling about relaxing your knees in a particu-
lar time at bat?

For a long time I thought something was strange, so I
checked it out in the mirror. That helped me get a mental picture of it. I actually tried it out in a game when we were playing against Anaheim. I knew then that I was on to something.

You've played baseball for more than twenty years, since you were a child, as a pro in Japan, and now in America, but it was only now, at this point, that you learned how to relax your arms, and your batting changed so much?

Batting changes over time. You think you've got it, then something gets out of alignment. It's a process of repetition. Your body changes, and so do your feelings, so it's only natural you're going to make adjustments. But making a major adjustment just indicates you're confused, so that's not necessarily a good thing. I don't think an adjustment you make after you've got your form set is such a bad thing, however. It's to be expected. I might make further changes in the future. It's certainly a possibility. But that's part of what makes the game interesting.

You often talk about keeping relaxed, making sure you don't get physically tense, and have said that you try to keep as relaxed as possible not just when batting but when playing defense, as well. On defense, then, crouching down in a set stance is not the ideal?

It's the exact opposite. It's preferable to just stand there than take up a kind of tense stance. But there is a difference between infielders and outfielders, since the ball's traveling different distances. Infielders can't just stand there; they have to get set to some degree. For outfielders, though, it's much better to hang loose than to get set like that.

It's interesting how we use our bodies. You can learn a lot from watching children. Adults tend to keep their bodies pretty tense. Especially people who've done some weight training misunderstand how to use their bodies. They try to oppose strength with more strength. But if you hit one hard thing against another somebody's bound to get injured. If you're relaxed, though, you can avoid injury. It all depends on whether or not you understand that. Like when you're making a catch in the outfield, if you know to relax when you hit the fence you can avoid getting injured. You often hear about how babies can fall down stairs without getting hurt—that's the principle involved. It's important for athletes to grasp this principle and learn how to use their bodies correctly.

For you, then, it was very important that you learned the principle that when you're batting you have to relax your knees in order to relax your hands.

That's the hard part. For instance, say your neck hurts, so you treat the neck and that doesn't help, and you discover the cause is actually in your back. In that sort of case it's easy to overlook the back. It takes a long while to pinpoint the real cause. The same can be said of baseball. In the setup I was describing, if you focus solely on the hands you won't solve the problem. It's interesting that the answer comes to you when you focus on the lower half of your body.

And the discovery that you should relax your knees also led to increased head speed.

Correct. If you're relaxed, your head speed will naturally go up. The tighter you are the less speed you'll get. If you put all your strength into your batting stance your head speed will actually decrease.

You made this discovery in September 2002; in April of the fol-
lowing year you worked hard at adjusting the balance between be-
ing aggressive and being patient, and addressing the issue of
having too high expectations; and by May, 2003 you'd made the
necessary adjustments and your batting average started to climb.
Your batting average remained in good shape, as you batted .389
in May, .386 in June, and .342 in July. From the end of August,
though, you struggled with a new problem. What was that,
exactly?

A lack of concentration. I was too attached to what I wanted
to get, trying too hard for results. I wanted hits.

Trying to reach 200 hits for the season produced this lack of
focus?

It did. We had pressure from trying to beat Oakland to get
into the playoffs, too, but the main reason was trying to get to
200.

Up till now you haven't viewed stats as being as important as
those around you have. It never seemed like you attached as much
importance to numbers as a goal. But you're saying that actually
getting to 200 did start to matter more and more to you?

The longer I played, the more important it became to me. I
think those who followed me could see this best. The fans want
me to get hits, and since I've been able to in the past, 200 hits
became a kind of benchmark indicating I've done well. One
hundred eighty wouldn't cut it. For the fans it's got to be 200.
And for me I think it's certainly attainable. If I perform up to
my capabilities it's a number I should be able to reach without

too much trouble. It's a nice, round number. With batting average, on the other hand, when you're in a bit of a slump you can just skip games to keep your average up. And I don't do that. That's why I don't care too much about batting average.

You wound up with 212 hits in 2003, only the third person in major-league history to get 200 or more hits in your first three years. In 2002, your second year, you got 208 hits, fewer than the 242 hits in your first year. The number of walks, though, went up from 30 to 68 and your on-base percentage was the highest in all three years. Getting on base is what the leadoff batter's supposed to do, so 2002 wasn't such a bad year, was it?

It wasn't. And neither was 2003, for that matter. You can't regret hitting 200 hits. I can't help it if the times I was in a slump stand out. But as the batter, I can't let that get to me. Each year was satisfying in its own way, and each 200-hit season means something different. Continuing at a high level is harder than getting to the top in the first place, and I really get a lot of satisfaction from maintaining that level. The expectations on me differed depending on the year. In 2001 there weren't any expectations placed on me from the American side. People just wanted to see how well I could do. In that sense it was easy on me. So if I happened to wind up that first year batting .300 with 170 hits, people here would probably have said something like "Hey, this guy did a great job." Once I got to the second year, though, they started expecting more. They wanted something extra, and since they saw me now as a mainstay of the team, the pressure I felt was completely different from the first year. So the stats I got the year there were expectations, and those during the year when there weren't any, mean something totally different.

In that sense, the 200th hit you got in 2003, in a game on September 20 against Oakland, must have really meant something since you got there by overcoming that pressure. I imagine it made you all the happier.

Of course. I've never cried before over getting a hit. That's how much it meant.

You cried?

After I got that 200th hit I did, when I went out in the outfield. You couldn't tell because I had on sunglasses.

You were delving into a deeper layer of baseball.

I'm surprised at the things I still don't know, which makes me want to keep on playing.

You said that when you were struggling at the end of August 2003, you felt nauseated. Was this from the pressure plus the irritation you felt at yourself?

That's right. During that time I couldn't get baseball out of my head. I couldn't stop thinking of getting a hit. I'd dream about getting a hit and then wake up and be disappointed it was all a dream. I experienced that because I'd reached a certain level.

You dreamed about getting hits not about suffering because you couldn't?

They were dreams about getting hits.

Most people's dreams aren't like that. Most of us suffer in dreams because we can't do something.

In my dreams I'd be really happy because I could get a hit, and then feel bad after I woke up and lost it all.

Do you think the pressure to get 200 hits will continue next season?

As long as I get close to that number. But I want to feel that pressure again—I enjoy seeing how I'll react. If I don't get to that level I won't ever experience it. I'm looking forward to it.

In the majors in recent years Wade Boggs of the Boston Red Sox got 200 hits seven seasons in a row.

It's really hard to keep it up like that.

Have the batting coaches ever given you any advice?

It's helped me a lot that they've let me do my own thing these three years. When I'm struggling, though, I want to communicate with the coaches and it's hard because of the language problems. But you know, when I was in Japan, too, I never relied on others even when I was struggling, and actually that helped me. There's a side of me that wants to work through difficulties on my own. That builds up confidence. I'm really uneasy about the thought of seeing myself start to depend on other people when I've having difficulties. It might work out to rely on others in Japan, but in the States people don't know my background that well so it's hard to get them to understand me. Things aren't so easygoing here, and unless I'm the kind of player who can work things out on my own, I'll be crushed down.

What sort of batting-related issues are you facing in the upcoming season?

Usually in the pitcher-batter confrontation it's the pitcher who takes the lead, while the batter is more passive. So one major point for me is to see how far I can reverse things, and take the lead, and get the pitcher caught up in my rhythm. If things go according to the batter's pace, then the pitcher starts throwing the ball where the batter wants him to. That's one of the strange things about baseball. As long as I can create that kind of situation, I think I can put up some pretty good numbers. It's less a strategy toward the pitcher than a question of maintaining your own rhythm and having your opponent do things at your pace—that's what's important.

You won't need a strategy to deal with hard-to-hit breaking pitches?

That's not really an issue. Being patient, though, is important. I never have a problem with being an aggressive batter. As long as I'm in good physical condition, then I can always bat aggressively. If I can be a bit more patient I should be able to do well next season.

Aggressive batting has always been your trademark. I remember your first at bat in your first All-Star Game, when you faced Randy Johnson. You were able to go for it and hit off him. I don't think I've ever seen you tense and unable to swing the bat.

As long as I feel I can hit, then I can do that.

Has your overall batting stance changed much during the past three years?

Since I started relaxing my knees they're straighter, so people might think I've gotten a little taller—compared to the way

I used to stand.

An inside-out swing is the fundamental part of my batting, but in the 2003 season I tended to turn my wrists slightly more clockwise. So one goal for me is to get back to the way it was before.

You mean your inside-out swing disappeared?

No, it was still an inside-out swing, but I was focusing toward the right and a lot of my hits went to right field. I'd like to get back to hitting toward center.

One of the characteristics of your batting is how smoothly you shift your weight toward your right foot, the one facing the pitcher. Among other major leaguers, Hank Aaron would be another who shifted his weight quickly like that. He batted right-handed, of course, so he shifted his weight onto his left foot as he hit all those home runs.

My teammate Edgar Martinez also is very good at shifting his weight. He bats right-handed and moves his right leg, his pivot leg, a lot. For breaking pitches he slides his right leg forward to get the timing right. So there are batters other than me who shift their weight like that, though it's not too common. Edgar and I might look different at bat, but actually we're quite similar. He's aware of the similarity. We watch each other hit.

Defense and Offense

During the three years you've been playing right field in the majors have you completely mastered the characteristics of all the batters and ballparks?

I wouldn't say completely, but it has gotten interesting. When batters get a hit to right, though, the man on first doesn't try to make it to third, so I can't enjoy making an assist anymore, throwing to third and getting the runner out.

No more chance to show off your "laser beam" throws?

No. Occasionally a younger player will try to get to third, and I'm happy to oblige. Recently I've started to predict better how a certain batter will hit and then I'll shift, say, a couple of steps to the left, and sure enough the ball will be hit right there and I'll be able to catch a ball I might otherwise not have gotten. That's a great feeling. To the fans it might look like a simple fly ball to right, but that's because I've moved beforehand. That aspect of defense has gotten very interesting.

When I see you play at Safeco Field it looks like you actually shift your position slightly for every batter, and for every pitch.

I did that a lot when I was in Japan, too. Say there was a really good batter at the plate—I'd move a couple of steps toward him. Superstar players have their pride, and when they saw me step closer they'd deliberately aim for right field. But never once did the ball get past me. What happens is they lose their temper a bit, try to hit the ball too hard, and end up popping up in shallow right. There's that kind of mental strategy going on between batter and outfielder. I don't know whether players in America view those kinds of defensive shifts that way, but they do in Japan.

Getting back to throwing, having a lot of assists doesn't

necessarily mean your defense is good, does it?

Lots of assists means your opponents are underestimating you. When the number of assists goes down that means the opposing team recognizes you have a strong, accurate arm.

I remember how at first you said the ball they use in the majors felt too smooth and slippery. How about now?

I'm completely used to it. In fact, a Japanese baseball feels strange to me now. The balls used in Japan are really high quality, but it's like they fit your hand too well, so when I throw one now I'm afraid I'll spike it on the ground. It's kind of scary how you get used to things. At first I couldn't control American balls, but now I think they're easier to throw.

You stole thirty-one bases in 2002, and thirty-four in 2003. You've stated that in the 2002 season you ran only when you were 100 percent sure you'd be safe, while in 2003 you took more of a risk and this percentage was more like 70 to 80 percent. In spite of this, the number of times you were caught stealing went down from fifteen to eight, almost half. Was there a reason for this?

In 2002 most of the times I was picked off were hit-and-run plays, or run-and-hit plays, not pure cases of being caught stealing. There were a lot of times when the count would be 3 and 2, I'd automatically take off, the batter wouldn't make contact but would go down swinging, and it'd end up a double play.

So it was more an issue of the batter. One of the areas where you said you can really excite the fans is in your running—base stealing and base running. Have you enjoyed this aspect of the game?

That's the part of the game that doesn't get easier, no matter how years I play. Defense and batting are difficult, too, but I've never had a time when I thought base running was easy. I have had quite a few periods when I think batting is easy, but I've never once thought that about base running.

What I mean is, I'm the kind of player people expect to move along the bases, so I have to. I'm a "super express" train, you might put it, that isn't allowed to stop, who's not allowed to make errors in judgment. On the other hand, there are some runners who are more like a local train that stops at every station, and that's no problem as everybody is aware of this. The tough part for the "super express" player is that he's always expected to move along the base paths. That's what makes it hard.

The batter hits the ball and it goes to the outfield. The decision, if you're on first, about whether or not to try for third depends on the condition of the grass, whether it's wet or not. If it's wet, then you risk it and round second for third. If the grass isn't wet and, in good condition, you hold up at second. You have to make that judgment call in a split second, in the two or three seconds between first and second, which isn't nearly enough time to make such a decision. But you still have to make the call, and that's what makes it tough.

When you say the grass is wet, do you mean games when it's raining?

No. Depending on the time of day the grass can get wet, but not because it's raining. Especially when we play in California, after the seventh inning the grass gets completely wet. That makes it hard for the outfielders to throw. You can't control the ball. In cases like that I round second and head for third, even if it's the kind of hit that you wouldn't normally try to stretch into two bases.

That wetness is something you feel when you're playing right field, too?

Sure. So if the ball just takes one hop and the outfielder grabs it, I don't go for third. If it's a grounder to the outfield, though, I have to make a snap decision. Grounders make the ball wetter.

So even in California, normally a pretty dry place, as it gets later in night games the grass gets that wet?

It does. In games in Seattle and on the East Coast, though, it doesn't. You particularly notice this in games in California, in Oakland or Anaheim.

Of course in tie games you'd do this, but you have to input all kinds of information—everything from what kind of arms out-fielders have to where they're positioning themselves, even the con-dition of the grass—and after the ball is hit make an instantaneous decision. That's got to be extremely difficult.

Also, when the outfielder leaps up and the ball grazes his glove, even if I watch when it's hit I can't tell right away whether he's caught it or not—no matter how long I play base-ball. But if I make an error because of a misread there, it's my fault. I'm supposed to do both: If they catch the ball I have to get back to my base; if the ball gets through I have to run and score. Not an easy task, believe me. It would be easy if the team had a rule you could follow that said in a situation where it's hard to decide what to do, where you think the ball might be caught, you could just stay on your base, but they want me to do both. That's the toughest thing about being a runner.

I've never seen any kind of silly running error you've made, or many times where you were thrown out because you'd made an error in judgment in base running. Do you remember any times you made those kinds of mistakes?

Hardly any at all, though I do remember one in the 2001 season. Chuck Knoblauch was playing outfield for the Yankees. Usually he played infield, second or shortstop, but that year they moved him to the outfield and he wasn't that used to playing that position. A blooper was hit in front of him. I was on second and thought he would just miss it. But he tried a sliding catch and caught the ball, and it turned into a double play. That's the only error I can recall.

Another time I remember was at the end of 2002, a tough time for the Mariners, when we were fighting Anaheim to advance to the playoffs. This was a game against Oakland. There was one out, a runner on first, and me on second. The batter hit a grounder just in front of first, which the first baseman had to run to get. They were going for the double play—the first baseman throws to second, who throws back to first, with the pitcher covering first for the third out. As I was running I pictured the pitcher looking down for the bag with his foot. Some pitchers can be sort of awkward that way, take too much time to touch the base, and don't get the third out. So I was sure I could make it home. What happened, though, was when the pitcher got the toss back from second he didn't tag first but threw home instead, and I was tagged out. This was my mistake, of course, but it was a calculated risk. We had to get another run in. At a time like that it all depends on whether or not the manager and coaches understand the player's intention. If they do, that's a big relief for the player.

So what about in this case?

The coaches all understood what I was trying to do.

If we just confine ourselves to these instances when you were thrown out, it sounds like you're not a very good base runner. Actually it's the exact opposite—your excellent judgment and base running score a lot of runs for the Mariners and have saved the team many more times than you've made base-running errors. For example, there was the game in 2003 when you faced the Atlanta Braves' star pitcher Greg Maddux. You got on base on an infield hit, stole second, then third, then the number-three batter, Bret Boone, hit a grounder to third, driving you in. That was a memorable run. I never imagined you'd try to score on a grounder to third!

Actually that wasn't such a hard call to make. A more difficult one was in 2002, in a game against the Toronto Blue Jays in Seattle. John Olerud was at bat and I was on third. We were in extra innings, and Olerud hit a grounder to second, driving me in, winning the game. The Toronto infield was playing in, so anybody would think on a grounder to second the runner from third would be tagged out at the plate. Our bench gave me the go sign, so I went for it. But if I had made a decision right after the batter hit, there's no way I could have been safe. I had to have a mental image beforehand of the kind of pitches this pitcher might throw to Olerud, what kind of grounder he might hit and where, and the timing of my start for home. You have to have a mental image of those kinds of things before they happen. The pitcher was a southpaw who liked to throw sinkers. I imagined the ball would be hit to either short or second. And that's exactly what happened.

Those times are the greatest. It feels good to hit a home run to win the game, for sure, but nothing could make a player happier than a case like this, where no one expects it, the infield's playing in, the batter grounds to second, and it looks like there's no way you can be safe at home yet you are, winning the game, no less. Those are the times I get emotional—when you have to make a split-second decision in a tough situation and score a run. My emotions just come out at times like those.

It's like a thrill running through you.

Yes, it really is. And it's something that only speedy runners can ever experience.

That's the whole point of baseball, isn't it, that you're out there to score runs?

It isn't that easy to hit, so unless you think about how to score when you're not getting hits, or, if you're on defense, how to keep the other team from scoring in ways other than getting hits, you won't be able to win close games.

Do you think this attitude of yours has made some impact on the major leagues?

I'd be happy if it did. The physical level of the game here is quite high, but for me, there exists a whole mental, strategic side of the game. People should know that even someone kind of small like me can make things happen by reading the situation and acting on it. If you start to pay attention to this aspect of the game it's a big plus for any team. It opens up all sorts of opportunities. I'd love for the Mariners to be that kind of team.

The kind of baseball where the whole team uses its collective brain power to try to win. By the way, in 2003 you got a new manager, Bob Melvin. I think he's a different type of person from your former manager, Lou Piniella, but do you think he's had the ability to manage a team that way?

It depends on how mature all the players can be. As long as they're a team full of mature players who don't wait for the manager to urge them on, I'm sure Bob can really show what he's capable of. If there are a lot of players who have to be constantly pushed, then they won't be able to see his thoughtful strategy, and that may be hard for the team.

So he's a manager who really thinks deeply about things.

Having been a catcher may have something to do with it, but he really does think hard about things, and understands what the players are thinking, too.

So he must be an easy manager for you to play under.

Very much so. I think he's a great manager. Two thousand

three was his first year as a manager, so I think he might have held back a lot. Maybe in 2004 he'll show a slightly different side of himself.

I understand that in the beginning of 2003, in April when you were in a slump, you told Melvin directly that he could take you out of the starting lineup if he wanted and you would even accept it if he sent you down to the minors. How did he react to this?

He laughed. He said he was never thinking of doing that, that I was a great leadoff batter and he wanted to continue to use me. He told me to forget about all that, and just go out there and do my best.

When you're not doing well it's very possible teammates may say something. They're pretty assertive and don't mind commenting about other people, so it's possible somebody might have said I should be pulled out of the lineup. At the time I thought the effect on the team would be completely different if I spoke out to the manager beforehand. If one of the players, say, were to go to the manager and ask why he was still playing me, he could tell them what I'd already said to him, and tell him how I feel about it; then that player would come away with a totally different impression. As one of the key players on our team, I was thinking how I could take a leadership role, and I think this is one way to do that. I really was thinking it would be OK to go to the minors. I never would have been able to say something like that my first year on the team. The first year I had to make it no matter what, and there was no way I wanted to be sent to the minors. But after two years on the team I was comfortable enough to suggest something like that.

Bob never tries to communicate something to the players through the media. That's a big help to the players. And he told the coaches to do the same. That's his way of doing things. That's the way you build up trust between the manager and players, the coaches and the players. It's not too pleasant to have to learn things through the media. You end up thinking, "If you've got something to tell us, tell it to us directly." Melvin always does.

Impressive Opponents

To go back to running one more time, when you try to steal bases now, which catchers do you need to watch out for the most?

In 2003 Bengie Molina of Anaheim was really good. So was the Yankees' Jorge Posada. There's no catcher who's easy to steal off of. Brandon Inge of Detroit isn't as well known, but he's amazing. I think he's on the same level as Pudge [Ivan Rodriguez]. I was really surprised by how good he is. He had some batting issues and was sent down to the minors in 2003, but his throwing is something else.

Did you try running on him?

I did, and I wasn't always successful. What really surprised me was how, when I was safe, even when I was sure of the timing and was 120 percent sure I'd be safe, it was always a very close play. Pudge was the same way. There are some simply amazing players in the U.S. I imagine even in the minors there

Balancing strength and patience at bat.

have to be some catchers who have fantastic arms like that.

How about pitchers? Which ones did you find interesting to face?

The three Oakland pitchers were, as always, tremendous: Tim Hudson, Mark Mulder, Barry Zito. Roy Halladay of Toronto is great, too. Esteban Loaiza of the White Sox has a tremendous cut fastball. It breaks a whole lot, and comes at you at 93 to 94 miles per hour. Anyhow, there are very few easy pitchers to face in the majors. In Japan there are, but here there aren't many at all you can feel relieved about facing. No—actually every team's pitchers here are tough.

Being in the same division as Oakland you played them a lot. Which of the three pitchers you mentioned was the hardest?

They're all hard. They have their own different style. Hudson really puts his heart into his pitches, and when it's really important not to give up a hit, he does what he can to keep from giving up one. He's tenacious and strong. With Mulder and Zito it's more that they pin you down with their pitches. Especially Zito has amazing technical skill. Hudson isn't so big, but you get a feeling of being overpowered.

He doesn't have a big windup, and he doesn't seem that tough, at least to the casual observer.

But when you face him, he throws some tremendous pitches.

In the 2003 season you were able to bat .359 against left-handed pitchers, which left-handed batters like yourself usually don't do well against. Is there a reason for that?

I have no idea. It's true I don't mind left-handed pitchers, not that I feel especially comfortable facing them.

There's a theory that when great left-handed batters face south-paws they keep their bodies closed more.

You mean it's harder to open up? I never had that feeling. It might really be the case, though. Maybe my body understands it. But it's not at a conscious level.

I imagine the experiences of the 2003 season, overcoming all those difficulties, will definitely be an asset for you in the future.

I'm sure they will. If I'd gotten only 199 hits I might have lost some confidence. I don't see how struggling to overcome those issues could be a negative thing.

Even when you were struggling you never forgot to take care of your equipment after each game—your gloves and spikes. I think people who are able to do that, able to keep to their routine even when they're struggling, are amazing. Didn't you have times when you wanted to chuck it all and go home?

I did. Some days I didn't want to do anything, not even take a shower. I just wanted to change my clothes and go home. I didn't want to see anybody. There were a few days like that. But if you do that, it makes it even harder to overcome whatever problem it is. The quickest way out is to keep to your rhythm and patiently maintain your routine.

You'd prepare for the games in the same way, too?

I'd try my best to. But my physical condition would change depending on the day, so I'd make minor adjustments to fit that.

Was the time you spent in the clubhouse taking care of your equipment also a time of reflection?

Of course. When you're cleaning your glove it's a wonderful time in which to reflect back on the game. As I clean my glove, I look back on the day and the game. I think that's time very well spent. I don't clean my glove just to get it clean, but to have some time to reflect back on the day and clear away whatever happened from my mind.

So you can leave baseball behind when you go home.

That's the ideal, to be able to shelve baseball away as much as possible before I go home. But it's not easy. A lot of times, when I don't perform well, I drag this all home with me. Still, though, even in times like those, cleaning your glove makes a difference in how you feel.

Do you write down any of the things you reflect over or think about, or technical things you notice?

Not at all.

Why not?

Because I'd never stay with it for long. And I don't like myself when I don't keep up with something. So it helps me a lot that other people write down things about me. I can see what my thoughts were about something. There are a lot of things I'll forget about. I'll probably be even more grateful for this in the future.

You've told Japanese children to take care of their gloves. Is this a message for American fans as well?

For American fans, and for American players, as well. Frankly it was a shock to find players playing at the highest level not taking care of their gloves and spikes. I was really kind of surprised, and disappointed. Japanese players have a much better attitude toward taking good care of their equipment. They care much, much more about their equipment.

During these three years have you changed the kind of bat you're using?

At first I used bats made out of ash, but now I'm using ones made of a so-called "blue ash." I was using blue ash bats in Japan, but I thought ash would work better in the climate here in the States so I switched over. And it did. But later on I tried using bats made of blue ash and they felt fine, too. Blue ash is a strong wood and bats made out of it last a long time. Even if ash doesn't crack, it starts to chip off where the ball hits it, so it doesn't have the durability of blue ash. Once I was no longer uneasy about using blue ash bats here, I went back to them.

Why do you use a bat that's thinner than other players' bats?

The first bats I used were like that, plus I didn't want the ball striking the bat in some strange place. I want to make solid contact. I'd rather swing and miss than have the ball miss the bat's sweet spot. Because you leave yourself the chance to make good contact.

The thicker the bat, the greater the chance you'll mishit the ball? When did you first start using that kind of bat?

In the off-season in 1992, the first off-season after I turned pro in Japan. I'd been using a similar type of bat in high school, and in '92 I changed the weight of the bat and the overall balance.

I understand as a child you imitated all kinds of different professional players. Was the inside-out swing of [Kazunori] Shinozuka (formerly of the Tokyo Giants) helpful to you?

As a left-handed batter, Shinozuka didn't pull the ball, but tended to get crisp hits to center or left. I think you can say imitating him made me what I am today. I wasn't aware at the time, though, that I was doing an inside-out swing. I just imitated him and that's what happened. It worked out well for me.

When did you become conscious of the fact that you're swinging on an inside-out plane?

After I turned professional. I hit like this in high school but wasn't aware of it. I started to be aware of it in the 1994 season, as I was getting 200 hits. I learned about all kinds of ways of batting and was surprised to find this one.

So we shouldn't ever downplay imitating great players.

That's right. A lot of times imitating them will give you the spark you need. Especially children, since their form isn't set yet, would do well to imitate different players.

But maybe imitating you wouldn't be so easy?

With the weight shift I do, I'd say it'd be pretty hard to imitate me.

But there must be lots of kids, both in America and Japan, who do.

I would think so. I don't lift my foot up as much as I once did, and my overall batting isn't as unusual as it used to be, but still it's pretty distinctive.

How about other batters in the majors who do well with a similar inside-out swing?

Well, on my team there's Olerud, who bats left, and Edgar, a right-hander. They both have a totally inside-out swing and can hit the ball anywhere. The opposite would be your pull hitter, someone like Rafael Palmeiro, who totally pulls the ball. Funny thing is, even though the pitchers know that, they still pitch him there and he ends up with around 40 home runs each season.

Does he depend more on things going according to the batter's sense of timing, like you were talking about before?

I think so. He's especially able to hit well against the Mariners. His swing looks so simple. Barry Bonds's swing doesn't look so simple, but when you look at Palmeiro it really looks like he hits the ball so easily.

What are your thoughts on training these days?

I mentioned how in spring training in 2003 I seemed to be hitting well but then, when the season started, I was in a slump. I've sometimes wondered what the whole point of spring training is. Camp starts late in the U.S., but in Japan it begins on February 1. I wondered what the point of it is. You do spring training but then things fall apart as soon as the season starts, so you go back to your old form. Then some opportunity comes along and you pull out of your slump. Makes me wonder sometimes whether we even need spring training.

In Japan they believe that unless you run and train hard in spring training you won't have a good season, but is that really the case? It's something we need to reconsider.

So you don't think the more training the better?

Recently I've started to think that after I get my batting up to par then I don't really need spring camp or any kind of preparation before the season begins. Of course running and physical training are necessary, and in the past I used to need at least ten to fourteen days of fine-tuning before the season. What happened, though, was that in January 2004 I swung a bat for the first time in a month and it felt fine. I didn't feel rusty at all. In the past, if I practiced batting after a month off my batting wouldn't be at all like my mental image of what it should be, and I'd have problems even getting clean contact off the batting-practice pitcher's pitches. But this time I was pretty much able to hit the way I wanted to from day one. So if you use your time wisely you should be able to do better. I don't need the satisfaction you get from lots of practice anymore. "No pain, no gain," as they say, but I don't feel that way anymore. Of course when you're young you need to go through something like that. But I wonder whether it makes any sense for me now. Every player's physical condition and emotions are different, so you really have to look at things objectively. I think that if you want to continue playing that may be the most important thing to consider. In other words, how to look at yourself as an outsider would. People like the feeling of satisfaction they get after they've done a lot of practice, but if you keep that up, then you won't have a long career. That's something I want to think about from now on.

Then if you want to think about having a long career, you shouldn't just continue the same exact regimen that got you to this level, right? Was this the first time you've had that experience that you felt perfectly fine swinging the bat after a month away from it?

It was. In the past I always wanted at least a week to get up to speed.

Playing for Enjoyment

During the season you've had to spend a lot of time playing games away from Seattle and may not have much time to enjoy life in the city, but I was wondering what you like most about Seattle.

I like the fact you can see water everywhere you look. I don't think you can find this kind of scenery anywhere else in the U.S. That's something very special about this city.

How do you spend your time off?

I don't go out so much, but I try more to enjoy doing things around my home. I've gotten interested in furniture and paintings recently, and have been collecting paintings and thinking of making my own furniture. During the off-season in 2003 I got interested in art and ornaments and have been going around quite a lot looking for them.

Do you paint?

No, I don't have any talent at all. I never even thought about doing it.

So you're trying to look for good paintings?

That's right. I like bold paintings with a lot of energy. Not the kind that draw you in so much. During the off-season I found a few like that. The paintings I look for in Seattle, antique furniture in San Francisco. It's really a lot of fun.

Are you still collecting signed baseballs?

After 2001 I stopped asking players to sign balls for me. That's just something I felt like doing in my rookie year.

In an interview you did in the off-season in 2003 you said that these past three years you've done your utmost to meet the fans' expectations, but from now on you "want to do what I want to do." What did you mean by this?

The fans in Japan have expectations in all sorts of areas, and even though I didn't need to be concerned about these expectations, I've been overly conscious of them as I've played these last three years. Even the kind of ridiculously high, out-of-line expectations some of them have. These are the kind of people who always say all kinds of critical things about my performance. The fans who really pay close attention to me, though, have sound standards, and those are the kind of fans I want to treasure. But I don't plan anymore to carry around with me the expectations of the kind of people you might not even call fans. That's what I meant in that interview.

I have my own ideas about the kind of baseball I want to play, and that's what I want to pursue. I'm not going to ignore the fans, of course. I'll always have them in mind. But my first priority will be playing the way I want to play. I don't know how the people watching me will feel about this, but I'm not going to be telling them how to watch me. Everyone can appreciate it the way they want to. The sort of style where they can enjoy watching me enjoy myself. Not me playing so they can enjoy it, but having the fans enjoy me enjoying myself. It's a shift in my way of thinking.

I've started to think that unless I do this it'll be increasingly hard on me, and the fans won't be happy, either.

I think my fans, especially in Japan, are really quality people. I started to get more fans in 1994 when I got 200 hits, then my fan base reached a peak when my team, the Orix Blue Wave, won the Japan Series, but this decreased in the years after that. When I came to America in 2001 the number of casual fans went up, but that's diminished somewhat over the past two years. I get the feeling those who are still following me are pretty determined people, and I can't ignore them. Of course I want to play up to their expectations. I want to tell those fans who've followed me all the way to stay with me.

How about American fans, the ones who fill Safeco Field?

American fans are different from Japanese fans. I haven't yet figured out exactly what they're feeling. I'm really looking forward to knowing more about them. What I can't express in words, because of the language barrier, I hope to show them with my performance on the field. I hope I can do that even more as time goes by.

And it would be great if the team wins and goes on to the postseason, wouldn't it?

That would be wonderful. I think the Mariners have it in them to do that. It's the kind of team that always has the potential of making it to the playoffs, the kind of team that can make the effort to accomplish that. And since that kind of great team thinks I'm an asset as an individual player, I really want to do what I can to repay them. I don't know if in these past three years I've repaid all their investment in me, but I'm confident I've made a contribution. I want to help the team win, of course, but also I want to be an appealing sort of player myself.

If you look at the past history of the team, in the 1980s and early '90s the Mariners had the worst record in the majors, and in the '80s, were the team with the lowest attendance. In all of pro sports in America, including the National Basketball Association, National Football League, and National Hockey League, the Mariners were the one expansion team that took the longest before they had a winning season. From their first year, in 1977, they had a losing season for fourteen years. But with some die-hard supporters behind them, the team grew stronger, and since the late '90s it's been a winning team. I'm really looking forward to you and your teammates taking this the next step and capturing the World Series.

During this off-season we were able to pick up some excellent players, and we have a very strong team now. If they and the existing lineup can really pull together, I have great hopes for the upcoming season.